The Hope of Things

The Hope of Things to Come

Anglicanism and the Future

Edited by
Mark D. Chapman

mowbray

Published by Mowbray
A Continuum Imprint
The Tower Building, 11 York Road, London SE1 7NX
80 Maiden Lane, Suite 704, New York, NY 10038

www.continuumbooks.com

British Library Cataloguing-in-Publication Data
A catalogue record for this book is available from the British Library

ISBN13: 978-0-5675-8884-5 (Paperback)

Typeset by Mark D. Chapman
Printed and bound in Great Britain by the MPG Books Group

Contents

Foreword by the Series Editor

Affirming Catholicism exists to promote education and informed theological discussion in the Anglican Communion. While it seeks to embrace the best of the catholic tradition it is not narrowly partisan and strives to encourage the kind of thinking that rises above the prejudices that so often characterize theological debate in the churches. This series of books is intended to provide resources for the Church as it seeks to move forward into the future.

Mark D. Chapman
Cuddesdon
The Feast of the Transfiguration of Our Lord, 6 August 2009

Notes on Contributors

Joseph P. Cassidy is Principal of St Chad's College, Durham. Originally from Canada he spent thirteen years as a Jesuit.

Mark D. Chapman is Vice-Principal of Ripon College Cuddesdon, Oxford, Reader in Modern Theology at the University of Oxford, and Visiting Professor at Oxford Brookes University.

Andrew Davison is Tutor in Christian Doctrine at St Stephen's House, a Permanent Private Hall of Oxford University, and Junior Chaplain of Merton College, Oxford.

Charlotte Methuen is Lecturer in Church History and Liturgy at Ripon College Cuddesdon, University Research Lecturer at the University of Oxford, and Canon Theologian of Gloucester Cathedral.

Martyn Percy is Principal of Ripon College Cuddesdon, honorary Professor of Christian Education at King's College London, and Canon Theologian of Sheffield Cathedral.

David Stancliffe is Bishop of Salisbury and President of Affirming Catholicism.

Introduction

This collection of essays offers a series of reflections, all of which – in very different ways – focus on linking the past, present and future. Each tackles that key historical problem from a different perspective and with a different emphasis. Some essays are detailed investigations of the nature and sources of authority in Anglicanism, while others are more worked examples of how the past interacts with the present as it shapes the future. The themes of Scripture, Tradition and Reason which are dealt with in this volume continue to be of central significance for all Christians, not least those Anglicans who stand in the tradition of Richard Hooker and the great divines of the past. Most of the essays began life as lectures given at two study days held at St Mary le Bow in London in 2008, one shortly before and one shortly after the Lambeth Conference.

What unites them all is an awareness that the church is a historical phenomenon, shaped by its context, but also shaping that context into the future. In many ways this is the problem that characterizes theology at its best; and it is undoubtedly true of the great writers of the Anglican tradition. Thinkers from Cranmer through to the current Archbishop of Canterbury have all sought to draw out from the Christian tradition resources which resonate with their environment, but which also challenge it in the hope that it might be reshaped in the light of that message.

Within the Church of England there is much talk of mission, of finding new expressions in which Christianity might be practised in the very changed circumstances of the present day: the influential report, *Mission-Shaped Church* has been much discussed and much criticized but it cannot be ignored. Fresh Expressions of church have been piloted; there has been a whole range of different experiments which have tried to make the Gospel more relevant to different groups, some of whom appear to be completely unchurched. No doubt these are well-meaning and honest efforts to stem the tide of decline and to ensure that as many people as possible hear the good news of Jesus Christ into the future.

There is, however, an inevitable danger with freshness and newness. It can perhaps dampen the enthusiasm for history which can appear rather stale and old. As a historical faith, however, Christianity is always an amalgam of the old and the new: the two live off one another. If Christianity has a past, present and future, based upon a revelation that happened at a certain time in a certain place and which was related to the past and to the future of a particular people, it would seem imperative for all Christians to re-assess the nature of history and tradition. It is not so much the question, 'what can we learn from history?' that is important, as the far more crucial problem of having to wrestle with history whether we like it or not. God may communicate in the present, but he does so only on account of what he has done in the past. The fact is that he chose to do it in the perhaps unlikely place of first-century Palestine. This means that if we cannot learn from history we cannot know the God of Jesus Christ, who is the God made known in history.

Ultimately this is the problem of tradition, of how the deposit of faith given once for all to the saints (Jude 3) is preserved and handed down to the present (1 Tim. 6.20). That process of transmission is a historical process, which takes place within an institution which was shaped by particular people and which gradually adopted structures of authority and a hierarchical order. Tradition and authority are intimately connected to one another, but both are inevitable consequences of the historicity of revelation. The big problems which have divided the churches over the status of those who hand on the tradition and the validity and finality of their interpretations are at root a question of the relationship of past, present and future.

As with other books in the Affirming Catholicism series, this book does not offer simple solutions to the problems facing the Church of England and the wider Anglican Communion and Christian Church. But it does offer a sense of hope.

'In the which the pure Word of God is preached and the Sacraments be duly administered': The Ecclesiology of the Church of England in the Context of the European Reformation*

CHARLOTTE METHUEN

The Romanists have very cleverly built three walls around themselves ... As a result, the whole of Christendom has fallen abominably. In the first place when pressed by the temporal power ... they have declared that the temporal power has no jurisdiction over them, but that the spiritual is above the temporal. In the second place, when the attempt is made to reprove them with the scriptures, they raise the objection that only the pope may interpret the scriptures. In the third place, if threatened with a council, their story is that no one may summon a council but the pope.[1]

These words were written by Martin Luther in the summer of 1520 to the Christian Nobility of the German Nation, encouraging the German Princes and magistrates to take the

---

* This article is based on a paper given at the Conference of the Modern Churchpeople's Union, 'Saving the soul of Anglicanism: the nature and future of the Anglican Communion' (Tuesday 8 – Friday 11 July 2008). It was first published in *Modern Believing* 50:2 (April 2009), pp. 5–20. The conclusion has been slightly revised for this publication.

1 Martin Luther, 'To the Christian Nobility of the German Nation', in: idem, *Three Treatises* (Philadelphia: Fortress Press, 1972), pp. 10–11.

reform of the Church into their own hands. Luther identified three major – and not unfamiliar – problems: the relationship between the spiritual and temporal powers, including the relationship between the Church and secular law; the question of who should decide the interpretation of scripture, and the question of who was responsible for calling a council – that is, the location of authority within the Church. How those questions were answered in course of the sixteenth century is essentially the history of the Reformation. How those questions are answered in the current situation of the Anglican Communion may well define the history of the Anglican Church in the early twenty-first century.

I begin with Luther on the grounds that it can be helpful not only to place our discussions in historical perspective, but also to remember that there have been many times in which people have felt that the ecclesiastical world as they knew it was crumbling around their ears. Violent conflicts surrounded the Reformation and the changes in thinking about the Church and the preaching of the gospel which grew out of Luther's critique. The violence of those reactions, which brought war to much of continental Europe during the latter half of the sixteenth and the first half of the seventeenth centuries, which embroiled England and Scotland in a civil war, and which, almost half a millennium later, still resonates in tensions between Catholic and Protestant, for instance in Northern Ireland, is a stark reminder that religion and religious change elicit powerful, deep reactions, because they deal with powerful, deep questions: questions of God and how we respond to God. As Hebrews reminds us: 'It is a fearful thing to fall into the hands of the living God' (10.31): fearful not least because the encounter with God challenges us to rethink how we have been used to think things are. The question of what faith means for the actual situation of people's lives lay at the heart of Luther's challenge to the Roman Church in the early sixteenth century. It is, I would suggest, also the fundamental question confronting us in the Anglican Communion today.

It is very noticeable that the debates and disagreements associated with the current crisis in the Anglican Communion have been surprisingly – alarmingly – thin on historical reflection. Graham James comments: 'Not to know our own history is a serious shortcoming for Anglicans, for whom history and theology are inseparable.'[2] This chapter seeks to offer a small contribution to that historical reflection. It considers the way in which the emerging Church of England responded to the questions of authority which emerge from the critique of the Roman Church put forward in the Protestant Reformation, and how those responses in turn shaped the Anglican Church as it grew into a world communion. It closes with some tentative thoughts about how these historical reflections could perhaps help us to proceed in our current situation. I take this approach, not because I believe that we can or should seek to read our answers directly from history, but because I am convinced that the way we approach questions of faith, reason and revelation in our present context is shaped by, and can therefore be illuminated by, the ways in which these questions have and have not been answered in the past.

The Continental Reformation

Luther's concerns in his appeal to the Christian Nobility were threefold, and each had a central ecclesiological aspect. The third of Luther's points was in many ways the simplest. Who could call a council of bishops which could command

---

2   Graham James, 'Resolving to Confer and Conferring to Resolve: The Anglican Way', in: Kenneth Stevenson (ed.), *A Fallible Church* (London: Darton, Longman & Todd, 2008), p. 78.

authority over the Pope and begin to right the wrongs of the Church? This question, rooted in the medieval conciliarist movement, points beyond itself to ask not only about the relative authorities of the papacy and the bishops of the Church – that is, to questions of primacy – but also to the relative authorities of the Pope, kings and emperor. Luther noted that the Emperor Constantine had called the Council of Nicaea in the fourth century; given the manifest failure of successive popes to act to reform the Church, he saw no reason why the German emperor might not call a council in the sixteenth. This approach sits somewhat uncomfortably with Luther's later two kingdoms theology, partly because Luther became less enthusiastic about princely reform in the face of princely opposition to his ideas. However, the idea that the prince or the magistrate should take reform into their own hands was adopted with enthusiasm by many sixteenth-century rulers. What later came to be called Erastian church settlements, in which national rulers are closely involved in defining the teaching and the affairs of the Church, were rooted in the conviction of secular rulers that they were primarily responsible for the health of their subjects' souls and therefore must, at the very least, share responsibility for the proper ordering of the Church. The declaration on human rights, or legislation such as bills to outlaw discrimination on the basis of gender, race or sexual orientation are arguably later extensions of this same principle.

Luther's first point – his denial of the distinction between the spiritual and temporal powers – had a double import. Firstly, it emphasized that clergy and religious should not regard themselves as closer to God by virtue of their ordination of vows, and, secondly, that they should not be exempt from secular law.[3] The theological basis of Luther's response to these points, often summarized as the priesthood of all believers, was to emphasize that whilst some people must bear particular responsibility for the preaching of the gospel and the administration of the sacraments, this task did not made them in any way more spiritual or closer to God, or exempt them from the normal rules and laws of society. The first and third of Luther's three walls thus raise fundamental questions about the Church's relationship to the secular context, and about where authority lies within the church.

Luther rooted his response to these points from scripture, and claimed authority to interpret scripture anew, a claim he made explicit in the second wall. Here his criticism was that the papacy claimed the sole authority in scriptural interpretation, whereas in fact the responsibility of interpreting scripture belongs to the whole people of God, or at least to all who understand the scriptures in faith.[4]

This is the principle of *sola scriptura*, and it rests upon two fundamental, if intertwined, intellectual assumptions: firstly, that scripture has one meaning, and, secondly, that that meaning is clear. The first of those questions warrants more attention than I am able to give it here. Luther's assertion of the second was very soon contested: a few years later Erasmus would deny that the meaning of scripture was clear, arguing that a consensus about the meaning of particular passages of scripture must be established by listening to different interpreters, both present and past. Erasmus criticized Luther's arrogance in setting himself up to arbitrate in this process: why should one man have any more profound knowledge of the

---

3   Luther, 'To the Christian Nobility of the German Nation', pp. 13–15; see also Martin Luther, 'The Babylonian Captivity of the Church,' in idem, *Three Treatises*, pp. 243–245.

4   Luther, 'To the Christian Nobility', p. 21.

true meaning of Scripture than anyone else?[5] That question reverberated through the Reformation.

The determination of the correct interpretation of scripture took on a particular ecclesiological significance with the drawing up of the Augsburg Confession in 1530, in which the Church is defined as 'the congregation of saints, in which the Gospel is rightly taught and the Sacraments are rightly administered'.[6] Understanding what it means to say that that the 'Gospel is rightly taught' is thus fundamental to the discerning where the Church is to be found. In Lutheran contexts, the Augsburg Confession, along with some of the writings of both Luther and Philip Melanchthon, collected together into the Book of Concord, came to function as the primary means of defining what that truth is. Having protested against the application of papal authority in the definition of the true interpretation of scripture, Luther effectively defined the true interpretation which was to be maintained against those with whom he disagreed. By the late sixteenth century, Lutheran hermeneutics and ecclesiology were intimately and explicitly intertwined.

The ecclesiological definition of the Augsburg Confession was not only appealed to by Lutherans. In his *Institutes of Christian Religion*, Calvin too defines the Church as the place where the gospel is truly taught and the sacrament rightly administered,[7] and the *Institutes* can be understood at least in part as a guide to that proper interpretation of scripture which

---

5   For Erasmus's critique of Luther, see: *Luther and Erasmus: Free Will and Salvation*, translated and edited by E. Gordon Rupp with A. N. Marlow (Library of Christian Classics 17; London: SCM Press, 1969), pp. 38–40, 42–46.

6   Article VII. All quotations from the Augsburg Confession taken from the Project Wittenberg edition: http://www.iclnet.org/pub/resources/text/wittenberg/wittenberg-boc.html#ac.

7   John Calvin, *Institutes of Christian Religion*, IV.i.9.

defines the presence of the Church. Later Reformed confessional statement would include discipline as a mark of the Church and take a harder line than Calvin himself did on the need for purity within the community, so that in many Reformed traditions, uniformity not only of preaching – associated usually with a confessional statement to aid in determining this – but also of moral practice came to be regarded as definitive for the Church.

The Council of Trent, with its affirmation of the papacy as the arbiter of scriptural interpretation,[8] also introduced a renewed focus on the proper definition of the interpretation of scripture within the Roman Catholic Church; at the same time it defined the teaching of that Church on several controversial topics. It is deeply ironic that Luther's criticism of the papacy for having assumed the authority to define the correct interpretation of scripture effectively came full circle, defining as the ultimate authority either the Pope, or Luther, or Calvin, or a particular confessional statement, depending on a person's confessional allegiance. By the end of the sixteenth century, churches in continental Europe increasingly functioned as what we might call 'hermeneutic communities', in which their theology – and with it the boundaries of the community – was defined by particular approaches to biblical interpretation, in a way that the late medieval Church had not been at all.

---

8 Council of Trent, 4th session (8 April 1546): *Second decree concerning the edition and use of the sacred books*: 'Furthermore, in order to restrain petulant spirits, [the Council] decrees that in matters of faith and morals which are relevant to the building up of Christian doctrine, no one should presume to interpret sacred Scripture, by relying on his own skill and wresting the sacred Scripture to his own senses, in a sense contrary to that which the holy mother Church – to whom it falls to judge of the true sense and interpretation of the holy Scriptures – has held and does hold.'

The English Church in the Sixteenth Century

In the English Church, too, Article VII of the Augsburg Confession was taken up into the Thirty-nine Articles, becoming Article XIX:

> The visible Church of Christe, is a congregation of faythfull men, in the which the pure worde of God is preached, and the Sacrarnentes be duely ministred, accordyng to Christes ordinaunce in all those thynges that of necessitie are requisite to the same.

How 'the pure word of God' should be defined was not entirely clear in the English Church. The Edwardian Church, the context within which the original Forty-two Articles were drafted, was developing a consciously Reformed theology, supported by theologians such as Jan Laski, Martin Bucer and Peter Martyr Vermigli. The broadly contemporary Edwardian homilies were intended both to define the 'pure word of God', and to put it into the mouths of preachers. Nonetheless, the two Edwardian Acts of Uniformity introduced as definitive, not a body of confessional writings or a detailed confessional statement, but the two Books of Common Prayer. Parish churches were required to possess, besides the Book of Common Prayer and an English Bible, not a confessional theological work such as Calvin's *Institutes*, but Erasmus's Annotations on the New Testament. That is, whether or not they used them, people were given the tools to read scripture and think about it for themselves, and not simply given a confessional statement which told them how it was to be read. This was true even on some of the most controversial matters, such as the doctrine of the Eucharist. The Prayer Book exhortations at the Lord's Supper (which remain virtually unchanged between the 1549 and 1552 Prayer Books) encourage an emphasis on the Eucharist as the spiritual eating of Christ's body, but no precise definition of the preaching of 'the pure word of God' in this or of other matters was laid down.

If this was true in the Edwardian Church, it became more even so in the church created by Elizabeth I's 1559 Settlement. What kind of church the Settlement created is something about which scholars disagree, not least because of the difficulty in gauging just how the 1559 Settlement was implemented. What does seem to be clear, however, is that to observers in its own era, the Settlement looked unmistakably Protestant, even though it did not follow any particular confessional brand of continental Protestantism. Apart from its rejection of the papal authority – which to contemporaries was conclusive – the Elizabethan English Church had a vernacular liturgy, offered communion in both kinds, promoted access to scripture in the vernacular, and had married priests. These practices meant that to the makers of ecclesiastical polity, it was recognizably not a part of the Roman Catholic Church. That it retained a high regard for liturgy and ceremonial and the threefold ministry set it apart from some – but not all – parts of Reformed Protestantism, whilst being entirely congruent with the practice of Lutheranism in much of northern Germany and Scandinavia. Its continuing suspicion of images and its counting of the Ten Commandments, on the other hand, looked more Reformed than Lutheran. Confessionally, Reformed and Lutheran Churches on the Continent were increasingly distinguished by their definitions of the Eucharist, although this was a technical theological question which probably only very few truly understood; on this point the drafters of the Elizabethan Settlement seem consciously to have left a range of possibilities open. However patchily the intentions of the 1559 Settlement were actually put into practice, and whatever ways people found of living with them, the Settlement made the Church of Elizabethan England manifestly Protestant. That English Roman Catholics generally also perceived it to be so can be seen by the moral difficulties they felt themselves faced with by the requirement that they attend services including Communion according to the Book of Common Prayer.[9]

That is not to say that the Church in England under Elizabeth did not consider itself Catholic, which it also and manifestly did. It was Catholic because it sought to uncover and live out the way the Church had originally been. John Jewel wrote that although the Church of England had 'departed from that Church which these men call Catholic ... we are come, as near as we possibly could, to the church of the apostles and of the old Catholic bishops and fathers.'[10] The imperative to seek out the truly Catholic Church also had the consequence that the Church in England must govern itself. Jewel conceded that the Church in England had 'sought to remedy our own Church by a provincial synod,' and that some said that this was impossible without the Bishop of Rome's commandment; however, 'unless we left him, we could not come to Christ'.[11] By leaving what was deemed the 'Catholic' or Roman church, the Church in England had rejoined the true Catholic church. Nonetheless, this was not a rejection of the Roman Church per se. Hooker wrote, although Rome stood accused of 'gross and grievous abominations ... yet touching those main points of Christian truth wherein they

---

9   See, for instance, the cases discussed by Alexandra Walsham, 'Ordeals of Conscience: Casuistry, Conformity and Confessional Identity in Early Modern England', in Harald Braun and Edward Vallance (eds), *Context of Conscience in the Early Modern Europe 1500–1700* (Basingstoke: Palgrave, 2003), pp. 35–38.

10   John Jewel, 'An Apology of the Church of England,' in J. Ayre (ed.), *The Works of John Jewel*, vol. 1 (Cambridge: Cambridge University Press for the Parker Society, 1848), p. 100.

11   Jewel, 'Apology', pp. 101, 103.

constantly still persist, we gladly acknowledge them to be of the family of Jesus Christ.'[12] As Jacob notes: 'Both Jewel's and Hooker's works mark the *via media* of the Church of England: catholic in that it believed itself to contain all the essentials of the Church of the early centuries, reformed in that it felt obliged to rid itself of some of the doctrinal and practical innovations that had accrued to the Church in the Middle Ages.'[13]

This apostolic shape was regarded as including the threefold ministry, as Cranmer commented in his preface to the 1550 ordinal:

> It is evident unto all men diligently reading Holy Scripture and ancient authors that from the apostles' time there hath been these orders of ministry in the church – bishops, priests and deacons.[14]

The Elizabethan Church maintained this order against growing opposition of those influence by Geneva who favoured the introduction of a model based on Calvin's four-fold ministry and more distance between Church and State. Initially, at least, the focus seems to have been on the retention of the threefold ministry, rather than on episcopal succession.[15]

---

12   Richard Hooker, 'Of the Laws of Ecclesiastical Polity', in John Keble (ed.), *The Works of Richard Hooker* (Oxford: Clarendon Press, 1841), p. 283.

13   William M. Jacob, *The Making of the Anglican Church Worldwide* (London: SPCK, 1997), p. 20.

14   Gerald Bray, *Documents of the English Reformation* (Cambridge: James Clarke & Co, 1994), p. 277.

15   The retention of bishops in the Edwardian Church, in the late 1540s and early 1550s, is probably best understood as a means of ensuring national coherence of ecclesiastical structures; at this stage Calvin's alternative model in Geneva would not have been well known, and in any case the challenges of ordering the Church in the city state of

Although episcopacy is central to the functioning of the Church in England, as exemplified by the oversight and responsibilities of the bishop defined by the 1603/4 Canons, the canonical requirement for episcopal ordination emerged only in the aftermath of the civil war, when the Preface to the Ordinal as it was printed in the 1662 Book of Common Prayer incorporated a *passus* which had not appeared in 1550, or even in the ordinal as printed in 1661:

> no man shall be accounted or taken to be a lawful Bishop, Priest or Deacon in the Church of England, or suffered to execute any of the said functions except he be called, tried, examined and admitted thereunto, or hath had formerly Episcopal Consecration, or Ordination.[16]

Geneva were different from those of introducing a national Church Order. National churches needed national church structures, and it is notable that not only the larger Lutheran churches, for instance in Scandinavia, but also the Hungarian Reformed Church and indeed the earliest form of the Reformed Church in Scotland all had either bishops or superintendents whose responsibilities were similar to those of bishops. Therefore, although the retention of the three-fold ministry in the Elizabethan Church almost certainly reflects the Queen's known aversion to Calvinist order, it is likely also to have been a pragmatic move which allowed the Church in England to profit from the fact that, under Mary I, Reginald Pole had been relatively successful in renewing diocesan structures. This is not to suggest that episcopal succession was not being discussed in the sixteenth century; Calvin, for instance, offers some very interesting arguments against using apostolic succession to define the continuity of the church (*Institutes of Christian Religion*, IV.ii.2–4).

16 The 1603/4 Canons, although they clearly envisage ordination by a bishop, do not actually require it (*The Anglican Canons 1529–1947*, edited by Gerald Bray (Church of England Record Society, vol. 6), especially Canons 31–34). The clause 'hath had formerly Episcopal Consecration, or Ordination' does not appear in the Preface of the Ordinal published by John Fell in 1661 (*The form and manner of making and consecrating bishops, priests and deacons* (John Bill: London

However, even with a new focus on episcopacy, parliament and the monarch retained authority over many aspects of the Church's life.[17]

Judith Maltby argues that the post-Restoration Church is less national than established.[18] The focus on the integration of the Church into national structures, remained an important aspect in defining the Church of England, alongside a concern to reflect on the significance of that national identity. Archbishop John Sharp, writing in 1686, described the Church as:

> the whole multitude of Christians throughout the world that are instituted into one society by baptism. But when we speak of a church of any single denomination, as the Greek Church, the Ethiopic Church, the Roman Church, the English Church or the like, we mean only some particular church which is part of the Church Catholic or universal.[19]

1661); accessed via Early English Books Online: http://gateway. proquest.com/openurl?ctx_ver=Z39.88-2003&res_id=xri:eebo&rft_i d=xri:eebo:image:154111-02:2). However, it is included in the Ordinal as published with the Book of Common Prayer in 1662; accessed via Early English Books Online: http://gateway.pro quest.com/openurl?ctx_ver=Z39.882003&res_id=xri:eebo&rft_id=x ri:eebo:image:51433:294).

17 For the role of episcopacy, see Judith Maltby, *Prayerbook and People in Elizabethan and Early Stuart England* (Cambridge University Press: Cambridge 1998), pp. 158–69. The continuing question over the necessity of episcopal ordination is illustrated by a comment of the eighteenth-century Archbishop William Wake, who wrote of the licensing of a Scottish Presbyterian to minister in England, that although he himself would not have given such a licence, 'I should be unwilling to affirm that where the ministry is not episcopal there is no church, nor any true administration of the sacraments' (L. Adams (ed.), *William Wake's Gallican Correspondence and related Documents* (New York: Peter Lang, 1988–91), vol. 5, p. 57).

18 Maltby, *Prayerbook and People*, p. 235.

19 John Sharp, 'A discussion of the question which the Roman Catholics much insist upon with the protestants, viz. In which of the

Within its particularity, writes his successor William Wake in 1718:

> The Ch. of England as a national Ch. has all that power within Herselfe, over her own members, which is necessary to enable her to settle her doctrine, Government and Discipline, according to the will of Xt, and the edification of her members. We have no concern for other Xn. Chs. more yn that of charity, and to keep up the unity of the Catholic Ch. in the Communion of Sts.[20]

The French Church, Wake suggests, could do this too, 'if it would in good earnest throw off the Pope's pretensions'.[21] In many ways, it seems that the unifying feature of the English Church was not confessional, nor even perhaps liturgical, although the Prayer Book certainly did play an important part in defining post-Reformation conformity, but a sense of the English Church as the Church of the nation.

The Church of England and the Spread of Anglicanism

The dominant English ecclesiological principle through the eighteenth and early nineteenth centuries seems to have been that of 'distinct families of nations which express the will of God in national Churches',[22] which shaped the joint Anglo-German Jerusalem Bishopric in 1841. In England, this expressed itself legally in the exclusion of 'non-conformists' and Roman Catholics from universities and government

---

different communions in Christendom, the only Church of Christ is found', in *The Works of the Most Revd Dr John Sharp* (London: Knapton, Longman etc, 1754), vol. 7, p. 96.

20 *Wake's Gallican Correspondence*, vol. 1, p. 100.
21 *Wake's Gallican Correspondence*, vol. 1, p. 100.
22 William H. Hechler (ed.), *The Jerusalem Bishopric Documents* (London: Trübner & Co, 1883), p. 32.

institutions. Mark Chapman suggests that 'virtually all the reformers were clear that power and authority resided purely in within the national church and nowhere else,'[23] but even in the sixteenth century, there was a significant difference the English Church and Lutheran churches: sixteenth-century Lutherans already had to deal with the fact that there was a plethora of forms of Lutheranism across the different territories; the Book of Concord arose as an attempt to define what made them all 'Lutheran', and did so in terms of doctrine. In contrast, although the Church of England was related to the other British 'Anglican' churches which emerged from the Reformation with their own distinctive features,[24] it nonetheless took shape as a somewhat isolated national Church until Anglicanism began to spread with the English colonists across the world. Moreover, when that expansion did begin, there was generally only one Anglican mission in any one place. Whereas parts of Africa and India experienced a German and a Swedish and a Danish Lutheran mission working virtually side by side, and had to work out the relationship of those different forms of Lutheranism to one another, the Church of England's missions tended to be less varied. Indeed, the particular biases of the Church Mission Society (CMS) and Society for the Propagation of the Gospel (SPG) meant that the spread of Anglicanism tended to be more theologically and liturgically monochrome than Anglicanism at home.

Anglican chaplaincies, parishes and dioceses, originally set up to serve the needs of English settlers, struggled with the same questions of dependence and independence as the

---

23 Mark D. Chapman, 'The dull bits of history', in idem (ed.), *The Anglican Covenant* (London: Mowbray, 2008), p. 92.

24 See, for instance, Jacob, *The Making of the Anglican Church Worldwide*, pp. 22-34.

settlements themselves, including the question of the relationship of these new mission churches to the Church of England. This began as early as the eighteenth century, when the American Samuel Seabury was consecrated Bishop of Connecticut in 1784, not by English Bishops – for Seabury could not take the oath of allegiance – but by Scottish Bishops, who were themselves proscribed in England in the aftermath of the 1745 Jacobite Rebellion.[25] Since Anglican mission increasingly sought not to export the Church of England, but to support the founding of distinctively Anglican 'national' churches in the colonial emerging nations,[26] Seabury's consecration was only the first of a complex set of developments which in the 1840s and 1850s gave rise to a series of Anglican Provinces across the world which were shaped by the need to give legal shape to emerging Anglican churches within emerging national structures and to define the relationship between local synods and bishops.[27] Consequently, as Chapman observes, independence came to be seen as the goal:

> Anglicanism has tended to display some of the triumph of national sovereignty and provincial authority, sometimes with little sense of the need for international regulation or mutual interaction. 'Mature' churches have been understood as those

---

25 Jacob, *The Making of the Anglican Church Worldwide*, pp. 66–68.

26 See, for instance, Mark Chapman, 'The Politics of Episcopacy,' in: Ingolf Dalferth / Paul Oppenheim (eds), *Einheit bezeugen: Zehn Jahre nach der Meißen Erklärung / Witnessing to Unity: Ten Years after the Meißen Declaration* (Frankfurt a. M: Lembeck: 2003), pp. 150–70; 167-8. This intention was compromised by the cultural imperialism often demonstrated by the missionaries: this problem in Sierra Leone, see Jacob, *The Making of the Anglican Church Worldwide*, pp. 200–8.

27 See Jacob, *The Making of the Anglican Church Worldwide*, pp. 105–43.

which can survive on their own without the need for assistance.[28]

Structures which enabled the autonomy and local flavour of emerging national churches and provinces left unanswered the question of how they related to each other.

This was already leading to tensions by the late nineteenth century, even at a time when most bishops of 'foreign dioceses' were themselves from the 'mother country' – England or the US. Theological tensions in South Africa and the protest of Canadian bishops were one reason for the calling of the first Lambeth Conference in 1867. Not all bishops attended it; not all were convinced of its legitimacy; not all knew why it had been called: 'disagreements over the purpose and authority of the First Lambeth Conference reveal that calls for definitive rulings, decisive moral leadership and a lack of provisionality in Anglicanism are certainly nothing new.'[29] Indeed, such concerns have been expressed in relation to every one of the Lambeth Conferences that has taken place since.

Lambeth 1867 was concerned primarily with establishing 'Union among the Churches of the Anglican Communion', and this too has been an abiding theme. Questions of organization, mission, permitted diversities of worship and doctrine, the relation between synodical and episcopal government, and the authority of the metropolitans (as the Primates were then called) were on the agenda of the first Lambeth Conference.[30] And these questions have appeared in some form or another on the agenda of every Lambeth

---

28 Mark D. Chapman, 'Introduction', in idem (ed.), *The Anglican Covenant*, pp. 8–9.

29 Mark D. Chapman, 'Where is it all going? A plea for humility,' in: Stevenson (ed.), *A Fallible Church*, p. 127.

30 Resolutions of the Lambeth Conferences can be found at: http://www.lambethconference.org/resolutions/index.cfm.

Conference since. In discussing these questions, one of the concerns of the early Lambeth Conferences was to ensure that the different Anglican jurisdictions did not come into conflict or competition, and that there were clear lines of communication, especially when it came to the consecration of bishops.[31] The principle which the Lambeth Conferences sought to implement was that of one jurisdiction in one place (assuming that 'no difference of language or nationality' existed) and the exercise of autonomy in the area of that jurisdiction. At the same time, they have sought to define and implement ways of working together, initially through the Lambeth Continuation Group, which met between the earlier Lambeth Conferences; later though the work of the Instruments established as a result of successive Lambeth Conferences, and especially the Anglican Consultative Council and now the Primates meeting. The efforts of successive Lambeth conferences have sought to define ways of working together so as to maintain the autonomy of the provinces whilst having enough definition to recognize each other as joined together in the wider communion. The current Covenant process is in many ways a continuation of that process, and the drafts of the covenant build quite carefully on the work of earlier Lambeth Conferences. We need to build on what we have, as the Archbishop of Canterbury noted in his response to the GAFCON statement calling the Communion together:

> It is not enough to dismiss the existing structures of the Communion. If they are not working effectively, the challenge is to renew them rather than to improvise solutions that may

---

31 Although a continuing theme, this is explicitly stated in e.g. Lambeth Conference 1908, Resolution 24.

seem to be effective for some in the short term but will continue to create more problems than they solve.[32]

Conclusion

All this is a plea to recognise that where we are now stands close continuity with places we have been before. James has commented on the alarming amnesia which exists in relation to these aspects of our history:

> Bishops at the most recent Lambeth Conferences seem to have been largely unaware of what their predecessors have resolved and taught. It seems a strange state of affairs for those who are bearers of tradition themselves.'[33]

We are facing a critical moment, but we are not facing any new questions. What is the relationship between culture and the gospel? Who determines correct readings of scripture? By what authority do we lay claim to truth? As Anglicans, our answer has tended not to be to resort to doctrinal statements, but to focus on how the richness of our diversity can manifest the catholicity of the Church. ARCIC has recognised:

> The Church's catholicity expresses the depth of the wisdom of the Creator. Human beings were created by God in his love with such diversity in order that they might participate in that love by sharing with one another both what they have and what they are, thus enriching each other in their mutual communion.[34]

---

32 The Archbishop of Canterbury responds to GAFCON statement, http://www.anglicancommunion.org/acns/news.cfm/2008/6/30/ACNS4417.

33 James, 'Resolving to Confer', p. 80.

34 ARCIC, *The Church as Communion. An Agreed Statement, August 28 – September 6, 1990, Dublin, Ireland*, London 1991, §35. For an

This diversity of traditions is the practical manifestation of catholicity and confirms rather than contradicts the vigour of Tradition. As God has created diversity among humans, so the Church's fidelity and identity require not uniformity of expression and formulation at all levels in all situations, but rather catholic diversity within the unity of communion. This richness of traditions is a vital resource for a reconciled humanity.[35]

That diversity needs to be taken seriously. As Kenneth Stevenson reminds us, 'Catholicity is about universality – but it is in denial of reality when it presents itself in static terms. There is a dynamic of tradition that is always going to create rough edges, where boundaries are pushed at and risks taken, in the belief that this is the (sometimes untidy) way in which the Spirit speaks to the Churches.'[36] What is necessary is to correct the failure identified by James – 'Our Communion fails to recognise how doctrine develops and Christian practice changes in relation to surrounding culture and new learning'[37] – and find ways in which this multiplicity can function as enriching rather than as detrimental. One way of moving in this direction is to move beyond assigning blame to understanding more of the diverse ways in which the gospel is being proclaimed and heard. Victor Atta-Baffoe has written:

> people lay the blame for the tensions and disunity either on the arrogance and theological liberalism of some churches (that is,

---

overview of the work of ARCIC see http://www.prounione.urbe.it/dia-int/arcic/e_arcic-info.html, with links to the ARCIC documents.

35 ARCIC, *The Gift of Authority. (Authority in the Church III) An Agreed Statement by the Anglican/Roman Catholic International Commission, Toronto – London – New York 1999*, §27.

36 Kenneth Stevenson, 'Communion and Conflict', in Stevenson (ed.), *A Fallible Church*, p. 154.

37 James, 'Resolving to Confer', p. 80.

those of the Global North), or on the biblical fundamentalism (that is, those in the Global South). Against this background, we fail to see the beauty of Anglicanism and indeed Christianity. Any attempt to define and enforce some universal Anglican norm or ethos brings with it the risk of denying the necessity of diverse, contextual ways of being Christian and doing mission. The beauty of Anglicanism is that there is no single way of being Anglican.[38]

This is not a plea for a smoothing over of our differences. We need to take seriously the fact that we are facing differences that seem irreconcilable. Global culture and the Internet mean that actions in one place of the Communion are more visible than ever before, and we need to be honest about how difficult that is to deal with. Stevenson has commented, 'There seems to be something singularly unattractive about parts of Western culture that motivate us to opt out of difficult situations, rather than taking up the challenge and actually working away at those disagreements.'[39] We need to engage with the differences between us, in honest recognition of how difficult they are.

Working away at what we disagree about means engaging with each other as people of God, and that can lead us into new ways of understanding God. Nicholas Sagovsky has suggested:

> It is a matter of faith, that when debates become deadlocked, in the very activity of mutual dialogue there will emerge a deeper and more truthful *koinonia*. Here we have to argue against the premature foreclosing of debates, against comfortable *koinonia*, … the illegitimate manufacture and imposition of consensus

---

38 Victor Atta-Baffoe, 'The Anglican Covenant: An African Perspective', in Chapman (ed.), *The Anglican Covenant*, p. 145.
39 Stevenson, 'Communion and Conflict', p. 146.

that is ultimately a failure of faith in God the Holy Spirit to lead God's people through the wilderness into all truth.[40]

This is not an easy process and it calls us to change. Gene Robinson has commented on the transformation which is required:

> You have a worldview that seems to work pretty well at interpreting reality – then bam! Something happens that doesn't fit into that view, something that your old worldview can't even explain. You're thrown into chaos and confusion and nothing seems certain any more. And then, little by little, your old worldview is reshaped to accommodate this new truth.[41]

The question for us now, as it was for the people of the sixteenth century, is of how that new truth is defined. I know how I think it is defined, but others know as well – and we don't agree. It looks set to end in schism (but let us hope not in war) unless we can find ways of talking across those certainties. As Mark Chapman has pointed out: 'Nothing will happen unless there is a recognition of frailty, fallibility, and humility by all those involved in the Windsor Process. Such vulnerability may not be fashionable, but a refusal to lord it over others even to the point of death is not without an important theological precedent.'[42] But no one is very good at fragility when they are sure that they are right.

I was writing this chapter as responses to the GAFCON statement were appearing on the Internet, and as events unfolded at the General Synod of the Church of England regarding its vote on the Manchester Report and the Measure

---

40 Nicholas Sagovsky, *Ecumenism, Christian Origins and the Practice of Communion* (Cambridge: Cambridge University Press, 2000), p. 203.

41 Gene Robinson, *In the Eye of the Storm* (London: Canterbury Press, 2008), p. 17.

42 Chapman, 'Where is it all going?', p. 138:

to allow the ordination of women as Bishops in the Church of England. We find ourselves in difficult and unsettling times, but the structures of the Communion may be stronger than they seem. After the 1988 Lambeth Conference, Timothy Dudley Smith commented: 'I felt the Conference has been a personal triumph under God for the Archbishop of Canterbury. I do not see how the British press can go on picturing him as an ineffective and isolated leader presiding over the dissolution of the Anglican Communion.'[43] Perhaps it is salutary to remember that this is not the first time that the press has constantly spoken of the Archbishop of Canterbury as 'an ineffective and isolated leader presiding over the dissolution of the Anglican Communion'. Fortunately, the Anglican Communion has proved much harder to dissolve.

As a theologian deeply involved in ecumenical dialogue, I am acutely aware of the ways in which different aspects of the gospel truly preached, which in the sixteenth century were divisive, are now been recognized and acclaimed in the dialogues and agreements between the churches which emerged from the Reformation. Division has been a part of the history of the Church, and for all the pain and wrongness of fragmentation, when division is about something true, we may indeed learn something about the gospel truly preached. This gives me hope that wherever the path we now walk takes us, we may be able to learn from each other, if not now, then later. At the same time, history points to the fact that we have and will come back again and again to the question of what it means to preach the true Word of God, and to how our reason and our context influence our answers to that question.

In 1898, the Churchmen's Union for the Advancement of Liberal Religious Thought – which came to be known as the

---

43   Vinay Samuel and Christopher Sugden, *Lambeth: A View from the Two Thirds World* (London: SPCK, 1989), p. 101.

Modern Churchmen's Union – was established to 'unite Churchmen who consider that dogma is capable of reinterpretation and restatement in accordance with the clearer perception of truth attained by discovery and research'.[44] Fundamental to that endeavour, although not explicitly articulated until 1931, was the aim 'to promote the study of the Bible according to modern critical methods, and to interpret its message in the light of such study'. Anglicans have resisted offering a confessionally defined answer to that question. This position has no doubt enriched our liturgical tradition and perhaps also our intellectual tradition, but it has made it difficult to know how we might recognize the central truths of the gospel, and or discern how to distinguish between true and false ways of preaching the gospel varying contexts. It has also left us with the danger that individuals are left to define truth, without being given much sense of how to do that. Perhaps one response is to take seriously the need to be better informed about the contexts in which not just we, but also others, live out the gospel, and about how we have dealt with such questions in the past.

For in the end, all this is about the preaching of the gospel, to real people, in real situation. However much we might easy and quick want answers to our questions and our demands for clarity, the history of the Church suggests that we are not going to get them. Looking back on the disruptions of the Reformation from a distance of 500 years, we recognize that the true preaching of the gospel was not found only on one side. The gospel truly preached encounters us in all the different churches that emerged from the Reformation, in the varying answers to questions of faith, reason and authority.

---

44 The MCU objectives as drafted by successive generations of its executive can be found on the society's website: www.modchurchunion.org/About/History/Objectives.htm#1898

Thank God. And should we expect otherwise? For, in the words of Rowan Williams: 'to be introduced into relations to Jesus Christ is to encounter what is not exhaustible in word or system; ... it is to step, not into definitive enlightenment, but into faith.'[45]

---

45 Rowan Williams, *The Making of Orthodoxy* (Cambridge: Cambridge University Press, 1989), pp. 17–18; cited by Chapman, 'Where is it all going?' p. 137.

2

Passing on the Flame: A Reflection on Tradition, Ecclesiology, and History

CHARLOTTE METHUEN

Tradition is not holding onto the ashes but passing on the flame.
(attributed to Thomas More (1477/8–1535))

Years ago, I remember reading a story in the 'Humour in Uniform' section of a *Reader's Digest* magazine. It recounted how a young army recruit and his colleague were asked one day to paint something right next to the parade ground. While they were hard at work, one of them knocked over the tin of white paint. They gazed, horror-struck at each other. And then one of them had a bright idea. They carefully measured out an exact square around the spilt paint, and painted it in.

Twenty years later, that young man returned to those barracks, now a general. And there, on the parade ground, was a recently painted, beautifully accurate, white square.

This story illustrates the down-side of how tradition is often understood. Tradition too easily becomes synonymous with those things that are done just because they have 'always' been done – whatever 'always' means. In congregations, tradition understood like this is 'the way we do things', which often means, the way the last vicar did things, or the vicar before last. It is quickly apparent that these sorts of traditions may not be very traditional at all: they are customs, we might want to suggest, rather than traditions.

On the other hand, tradition is a powerful source of identity. Those soldiers, quick-thinking in their response to a critical situation, were also standing in a tradition. Their regiment will have had traditions of honour and courage which supported them at critical moments in battle. Churches and congregations too are shaped by tradition. Christians speak of standing in the Anglican tradition, the Catholic tradition, the Reformed tradition, the Baptist tradition. Roman Catholics and Orthodox have a strong sense of tradition as a living manifestation of the way in which the Holy Spirit has guided the Church through the centuries, giving rise to authoritative traditions which give the Church its identity. However, even churches which would not value tradition explicitly in this way are not free from tradition. Tradition – from the Latin *traditio*, to hand over, to pass on – is that which gives us identity; it is that which we value enough about the way we think about how we live our Christian faith to pass on from one generation to the next, one person to the next. Tradition, suggests Henry Chadwick, 'means the memory of the community which gives the people of God their self-understanding'.[1] Tradition is what helps us to understand that and how we exist in continuity with other believers, all the way back through the history of the Church to the first apostles. Tradition, then, helps us to grasp the important truth that the Church does not consist just of ourselves, here and now, but of all people who profess the name of Christ, in all times and in all places.

Anglicans, Catholics, and Tradition

Anglicans are accustomed to thinking of tradition alongside scripture and reason as sources of authority within the Church. For Hooker, tradition, strictly defined, is related to the *adiaphora* or matters indifferent to salvation, and it is defined by the Church:

---

1   Henry Chadwick, 'Ministry and Tradition', in idem, *Tradition and Exploration: Collected Papers on Theology and the Church* (Norwich: The Canterbury Press, 1994), pp. 12–18; here p. 14.

we mean by traditions, ordinances made in the prime of Christian religion, established with that authority which Christ hath left to his Church for matters indifferent, and in that consideration requisite to be observed, till like authority see just and reasonable cause to alter them.[2]

Submitting questions of order to questions of doctrine,[3] Hooker affirms tradition as subordinate to scripture, concluding:

What scripture doth plainly deliver, to that the first place both of credit and obedience is due; the next whereunto is whatsoever any man can necessarily conclude by force of reason; after those the voice of the Church succeedeth.[4]

However, in an age in which individuals felt empowered to interpret scripture for themselves, Hooker was wary of the waywardness of personal approaches to scripture, arguing that the external form of religion (and here his particular concern was the ordering of the ministry) should concur both with reason and be 'allowed fit in the judgement of antiquity and by the long continued practice of the whole Church'.[5] Those who do 'nothing but that which men of account have done before

---

2   Richard Hooker, *Laws of Ecclesiastical Polity*, V.lxv.2. For Hooker's views on tradition, and some of the disagreements about interpreting them, see Nigel Atkinson, *Richard Hooker and the Authority of Scripture, Tradiiton, and Reason: Reformaed Theologian of the Church or England?* (Carlisle: Paternoster Press, 1997), and Lee W. Gibbs, 'Richard Hooker's *Via Media* Doctrine of Scripture and Tradition', in *Harvard Theological Review* 95 (2002), pp. 227–235.

3   'Laws touching matter of order are changeable, by the power of the Church; articles concerning doctrine not so' (Hooker, *Laws of Ecclesiastical Polity*, V.viii.2).

4   Hooker, *Laws of Ecclesiastical Polity*, V.viii.2.

5   Hooker, *Laws of Ecclesiastical Polity*, V.vii.1.

them, are, although they do amiss, yet the less faulty'.[6] On the
other hand, Hooker was also adamant that

> all things cannot be of ancient continuance, which are
> expedient and needful for the ordering of spiritual affairs, but
> the Church being a body which dieth not hath always power, as
> occasion requireth, no less to ordain that which never was, than
> to ratify what hath been before.[7]

That is, on order to live, the Church may need to break away
from what has gone before.

The danger, which was recognized with deep intensity in the
sixteenth century, is that the awareness of the importance of a
deep sense of tradition becomes associated with the familiarity
of the customary 'this is what we do' in a way that is
stultifying. That is, there is a risk that tradition comes to be –
as Yves Congar has warned that it too often is – 'a collection
of time-honoured customs, accepted, not on critical grounds,
but merely because things have always been so, because "it has
always been done"'.[8] This is particularly likely to happen if
tradition is viewed as something monolithic, fixed and
unchanging, or when it is seen as a deposit to be preserved at
all costs. In this view, as it was put in the *Catholic Encyclopedia*
of 1908, 'traditional truth was confided to the Church as a
deposit which it would guard and carefully transmit as it had
received it without adding to it or taking anything away'.[9] The
Encyclopedia wanted to argue that this is not the full

---

6   Hooker, *Laws of Ecclesiastical Polity*, V.vii.3.

7   Hooker, *Laws of Ecclesiastical Polity*, V.viii.1.

8   Yves Congar, *Tradition and the Life of the Church* (London: Burns &
     Oates 1964), p. 7. [Reprinted as *The Meaning of Tradition* (San
     Francisco: Ignatius Press 2004).] For a discussion of Congar's
     understanding of tradition, see Aidan Nichols OP, *Yves Congar*
     (Wilton CT: Morehouse-Barlow, 1989), especially pp. 26–51.

9   www.newadvent.org/cathen/15006b.htm (accessed 13.07.09).

understanding of tradition, but the idea of tradition as a deposit is one which is still not infrequently held. The risk is, Congar suggests, that when tradition is understood to be fixed and unchanging, it will be used to stand firm against any change whatsoever:

> Any attempt at innovation is opposed in the name of tradition, which is considered first and foremost as a conservative force in society, and a safeguard against a dangerous liking for novelty, or even against any suggestion of a wider outlook. Tradition is favoured because it prevents change.[10]

Understood this way, tradition is primarily about preservation, about guarding what has been given and ensuring that it is passed on. Only in this way, runs the argument, is it possible to ensure the Church's continuity with the past; only so can the Church be sure that it is truly apostolic.

One major problem an understanding of tradition as a deposit or a body of propositions, or even a fixed set of practices, is the way in which it fails to understand the life which is central to the gospel. Commenting on the definition of tradition as a deposit confided to the Church, the *Catholic Encyclopedia* goes on:

> This deposit in fact is not an inanimate thing passed from hand to hand; it is not, properly speaking, an assemblage of doctrines and institutions consigned to books or other monuments. Books and monuments of every kind are a means, an organ of transmission, they are not, properly speaking, the tradition itself. To better understand the latter it must be represented as a current of life and truth coming from God through Christ and through the Apostles to the last of the faithful who repeats his creed and learns his catechism.[11]

---

10   Congar, *Tradition and the Life of the Church*, p. 7.
11   http://www.newadvent.org/cathen/15006b.htm

Whilst repeating the creed and learning the catechism may not be the best definition of the epitome of tradition (a question to which we will return below), the understanding of the tradition as enabling the transmission or passing on – the *traditio* – of 'current of life and truth' contained in the gospel message to the Church in every age and in every time is an important one. As Congar suggests, '[tradition] is a handing over of salvation, of the Christian life, of the reality of the covenant'; it implies not only a communication of the law, but also the communication of 'the Word in whom we are given life and the forgiveness of sins'.[12] In other words, as the ARCIC document, *The Gift of Authority*, puts it, tradition 'is a dynamic process, communicating to each generation what was delivered once for all to the apostolic community'.[13] This is not simply about passing down some kind of 'storehouse of doctrine and ecclesial decisions';[14] rather, tradition is 'a channel of the love of God, making it accessible in the Church and in the world today ... a treasure to be received by the people of God and a gift to be shared with all humanity.'[15]

That treasure is rooted in scripture. It is shaped by our understanding of apostolic tradition, and in particular, suggests *The Gift of Authority*, through the bringing of children for baptism, joint confession of the apostolic faith, celebration of the Eucharist, and leadership by an apostolic ministry.

(accessed 13.07.09).

12 Yves Congar, *Tradition and Traditions: An Historical and a Theological Essay* (London: Burns & Oates, 1966), pp. 279–280.

13 ARCIC, *The Gift of Authority. Authority in the Church III. An Agreed Statement by the Anglican/Roman Catholic International Commission (ARCIC)* (London: Catholic Truth Society, 1999) [hereafter TGOA], §14.

14 TGOA, §14.

15 TGOA, §15.

However, it must also be shaped by the recognition that these are gifts 'which must be constantly received anew'.[16] On the one hand, 'the Church must continue faithful so that the Christ who comes in glory will recognise in the Church the community he founded' – that is, as Christians today, we have a responsibility to ensure that we stand in continuity with those who have gone before us, recognizing that it is they who give us access to the faith. On the other hand, and at the same time, the Church 'must continue to be free to receive the apostolic Tradition in new ways according to the situations by which it is confronted'.[17] That is to say, we may expect that the tradition that we receive should and must be expressed in new ways in each generation.

There is, therefore, a tension in the way in which tradition mediates the past to the present. For although the apostolic commission is rooted in the past, in the moment of incarnation of Christ, in the life of the Church as it has been, in ways that cannot be changed; it is also, and always, rooted in the present; and looking towards the future. Thus Congar writes that tradition 'is the permanence of the past in the present, form the heart of which it prepares the future'.[18] That permanence cannot be static, but will be shaped anew in each generation, and that too is part of the tradition of the Church. 'True tradition', suggests Congar, 'is not servility but fidelity.'[19] As Eamon Duffy writes, the history of the Church offers 'abundant evidence that change, not stasis, is the sign of life'.[20] Similarly, Chadwick suggests:

---

16 TGOA, §16.
17 TGOA, §24.
18 Congar, *Tradition and the Life of the Church*, p. 107.
19 Congar, *Tradition and the Life of the Church*, p. 8.
20 Eamon Duffy, *Faith of our Fathers: Reflections on Catholic Tradition* (London: Continuum, 2004), p. x.

A church which is imprisoned in its own past will end by betraying the deposit of faith entrusted by God. A society "without the means of change is without the means of its conservation" (Edmund Burke, 1790). "To live is to change" (John Henry Newman, 1845).[21]

Chadwick affirms, therefore, that the ordained ministry – and with it the Church – 'does not exist exclusively to mediate and to transmit faithfully what has been received from a sacred past. It is also called to proclaim, to utter prophecy in the Spirit, speaking to a changing situation.'[22] Tradition, if it is to pass on the flame of the living gospel, cannot simply preach what has been done before.

The poet and theologian Kathleen Norris observes of her neighbours in a small town community in South Dakota: 'In forsaking the ability to change, they diminish their capacity for hope.' A return to the past may seem safer: 'What we need, my friend suggested, is to turn back the clock to the way things were twenty years ago, when the town was booming and the world made sense. There was nothing that could not be judged by the values we all shared.' Such an idyllic view of the past is tempting, but, suggests Norris, 'she may find ... that disconnecting from change does not recapture the past. It loses the future.'[23] This is true not least because the quest to recapture the past is impossible: to do 'what has always been done' in a new context is not in fact to return to the way things were, but to do something new.

---

21 Chadwick, 'Ministry and Tradition', p. 15.
22 Chadwick, 'Ministry and Tradition', p. 15.
23 Kathleen Norris, *Dakota: A Spiritual Geography* (Boston / New York: Houghton Mifflin, 1993), p. 64.

Tradition and Apostolicity

The Church is apostolic precisely because the gospel message of hope demands to be proclaimed in every generation, in every context. In finding the language that speaks to each generation, each context, tradition is woven and becomes more complex. Therefore, as the *The Gift of Authority* has noted, the tradition of the Church is intimately linked to its catholicity: 'In the rich diversity of human life, encounter with the living Tradition produces a variety of expressions of the Gospel.' [24] The Church, as it seeks to be true to its nature to be both Catholic and Apostolic, as it searches out what it means to be One and Holy, encounters, and becomes involved in shaping, living tradition. Whilst deeply aware of its rootedness in the past, it must proclaim a message to the present, looking to the promised future which is yet to come, to the Kingdom which is near by us but not yet here. On this reading, just as providence, the *providentia Dei*, has often been seen as *creatio continua*, that is, as the locus of God's continued act of creation in the world,[25] apostolic tradition, the *traditio apostolica*, may be better understood as *revelatio continua*, the locus of God's continued revelation to God's people.[26]

To stand in the tradition of the Church, then, is to take seriously the apostolic imperative. As the 1938 Doctrine Report of the Church of England puts it:

---

24 TGOA, § 27.

25 This connection is quite commonly made. See, for instance, Tyron Inbody, *The Faith of the Christian Church: an Introduction to Theology* (Grand Rapids: Eerdmans, 2005), 124–127; Christoph Schwöbel, *Gott in Beziehung: Studien zur Dogmatik* (Tübingen: Mohr Siebeck, 2002), pp. 146–148.

26 The term 'continuing revelation' is associated with tradition also by David Brown, *Tradition and Imagination: Revelation and Change* (Oxford: Oxford University Press, 1999), ch. 3.

The Church may also be called apostolic as being charged with to mission to bear witness to Christ and to declare His Gospel before the world. ... By its apostolicity, therefore, the Church of to-day is linked with the church of primitive times through an essential identity of doctrine, a continuity of order, and a fellowship in missionary duty.[27]

The Gift of Authority suggests that the central challenge in discovering the authenticity of tradition is to discern the faithfulness of its expression to 'the Word revealed in Jesus Christ and transmitted by the apostolic community'.[28] In the Anglican context, the Lambeth Quadrilateral, as accepted by the Lambeth Conference of 1888, has played an important role in shaping the definition of that faithfulness:

That, in the opinion of this Conference, the following articles supply a basis on which approach may be by God's blessing made towards home reunion:

a. The Holy Scriptures of the Old and New Testaments, as 'containing all things necessary to salvation', and as being the rule and ultimate standard of faith.

b. The Apostles' Creed, as the baptismal symbol; and the Nicene Creed, as the sufficient statement of the Christian faith.

c. The two sacraments ordained by Christ himself – Baptism and the Supper of the Lord – ministered with unfailing use of Christ's words of institution, and of the elements ordained by him.

d. The historic episcopate, locally adapted in the methods of its administration to the varying needs of the nations and peoples called of God into the unity of his Church.[29]

---

27 *Doctrine in the Church of England (1938): the report of the Commission on Christian Doctrine appointed by the Archbishops of Canterbury and York* (London: SPCK, reprinted 1982), p. 111.

28 TGOA, § 27.

29 http://www.lambethconference.org/resolutions/1888/1888-11.cfm (accessed 10.07.09).

This definition of apostolic faith underlies that offered by *The Gift of Authority*: the treasure which we have to impart is rooted in scripture; it is shaped by our understanding of apostolic tradition, and in particular, through the bringing of children for baptism, joint confession of the apostolic faith, celebration of the Eucharist, and leadership by an apostolic ministry.[30] The first three paragraphs of the Quadrilateral have largely met with agreement in ecumenical conversations; however, although there is wide agreement that a properly authorized and recognized ministry is imperative for ensuring the continued apostolic teaching of the Church, the historical episcopate remains a barrier to full interchangeability of ministries in some of the Anglican Communion's ecumenical conversations, although important steps have been taken through the recognition that *espiskope*, or oversight, is exercised in those churches which do not stand in tradition of the historical episcopate.[31] Important criteria for defining authentic, apostolic tradition have emerged from ecumenical dialogues.

---

30 TGOA, § 14, and compare also ARCIC, *Church as Communion*, 15, 43. Similar statements are found in many other ecumenical agreements. See, for instance, *The Porvoo Statement*, Section 3: 'What we agree in Faith', §§29–33.

31 Thus the Covenant between the Church of England and the Methodist Church of Great Britain affirms, 'that both our churches embody the conciliar, connexional nature of the Church and that communal, collegial and personal oversight (*episkope*) is exercised within them in various forms', and 'that there already exists a basis for agreement on the principles of episcopal oversight as a visible sign and instrument of the communion of the Church in time and space' [Anglican Methodist Covenant, §§ 6–7]. Similarly, the Meissen agreement between the Church of England and the Evangelische Kirche in Deutschland (German Protestant Church), while recognizing 'that personal and collegial oversight (*episkope*) is embodied and exercised in our churches in a variety of forms, episcopal and non-episcopal, as a visible sign of the Church's unity

Or would it? The current situation of the Anglican Communion points to the way in which different people may entirely agree on fundamental principles – for instance, that the Church's teaching must be rooted in scripture – whilst entirely disagreeing on what that actually means. 'Rooted in scripture' for some people means a particular reading of certain biblical texts referring to homosexual behaviour as valid in all places and at all times; for others it means a contextualization of those texts, a privileging of and understanding of the gospel as affirming covenanted relationships rooted in love, and a strong belief that one central message of the gospel is to preach justice for all who are created in the image of God.[32] Both appeal to scripture, in entirely different ways. Arguably, both appeal to scripture in ways that earlier generations might not have done. Brown (writing before the current crisis) believes that such tensions are inevitable, warning against associating claims to apostolic continuity with the reading of texts in any simple way. Although 'we assume continuity of text means continuity of content', he observes, the meaning of any given

---

and continuity in apostolic life, mission and ministry', can only sound a note of hope for the future in relation to the recognition of ministries: 'we acknowledge one another's ordained ministries as given by God and instruments of his grace, and look forward to the time when the reconciliation of our churches makes possible the full interchangeability of ministers' (Meissen Agreement, §VI.17.A.iii–iv). An almost identical formulation is found in the Reuilly Declaration, between the British and Irish Anglican Churches and the Reformed and Lutheran Churches in France (§a.iv-vi).

32 See, for instance, Desmond Tutu's introduction to Vanessa Baird, *Sex, Love & Homophobia: Lesbian, Gay, Bisexual and Transgender Lives* (London: Amnesty International, 2004), p. 5. 'We struggled against apartheid in South Africa, supported by people the world over, because black people were being blamed and made to suffer for something we could do nothing about; our very skins ... It is the same with sexual orientation. It is a given.'

text is in fact profoundly contextual, so that 'even the stories of scripture themselves have not stood still.'[33] Brown sees this recognition as a strong incentive to abandon 'the "deposit" view of revelation which has so dominated most of the history of Christianity' and move to a new understanding of continuous revelation: 'we may view God as constantly interacting with his people throughout history, and in a way which takes their humanity and their conditionedness with maximum seriousness.'[34] For Brown then, the reading and interpretation of scripture itself is subject to the same kind of provisos which have been raised above with respect to tradition; indeed, he maintains that 'revelation is mediated to the community of faith through a continuous stream of developing tradition'.[35] Apostolic tradition is not a fixed entity that the Church has been given to pass on, but something with which those who receive the gospel engage, and by which, through that process of engagement they are shaped and formed. Tradition – the lived reception of the gospel – thus shapes and forms the Church as well as being passed on by it. The Church as the whole people of God is engaged in the making of tradition as each person wrestles with what God is calling them to do. Brown can affirm 'continuing human reflection as itself an indispensible part of the process of divine disclosure',[36] it is the process of our own lived engagement which shapes received and lived revelation, and with it tradition, in any given context, in its turn forming a basis for the reception of revelation by the next generation.

---

33 Brown, *Tradition and Imagination*, pp. 5–6.
34 Brown, *Tradition and Imagination*, p. 107.
35 Brown, *Tradition and Imagination*, p. 169.
36 Brown, *Tradition and Imagination*, p. 169.

Tradition and History

The particular historical moment of reception is thus not incidental. Philip Sheldrake has observed that, corresponding to the use of the language of 'signs of the times' at the Second Vatican Council, there has been a shift in the perception of the relationship between history and faith, such that history can no longer be considered 'an accidental and extraneous fact' when considering faith. Rather, 'every historical moment has a dynamic of its own which is of value and a place where the imminent presence of the Kingdom of God may be perceived'.[37] Sheldrake sees this as the end of the subordination of historical facts to orthodoxy: 'Firstly, the recognition of history and the location of faith within it ... meant a renewal of true historical memory ... Secondly, a respect for history makes it impossible to reduce diversity and plurality to certain universal formulae.'[38] It is no coincidence that Congar's reassessment of tradition is closely related to this shift in understanding the relationship between history and faith.

It has often been noticed that the theology of Vatican II is associated with an ecclesiological shift within Roman Catholicism to take the laity more seriously as constitutive of the Church, arguably producing an ecclesiology closer to that taught by Protestant churches. Taken together with the growing awareness of historical context of the locus of reception of revelation, this shift ensures that understandings of the tradition of the Church must necessarily become more complex. A parallel – and not unrelated – development has seen historians themselves become more interested in questions of religion rather than theology, in tracing the history of the whole people of God rather than of those who

---

37 Philip Sheldrake, *Spirituality and History: Questions of Interpretation and Method* (London: SPCK, revised edition 1995), p. 37.
38 Sheldrake, *Spirituality and History*, p. 37.

sought to define belief and practice. Social history, histories of personal piety and practice, histories of the engagement of women with religion: all these have opened up the possibility of tracing traditions of faith which enable us better to sense the true complexity of what has shaped our churches today. Deepening our awareness of the complexities of the past may help us guard also against the danger of equating our own situation with that of our forebears, as Rowan Williams has suggested:

> Good historical writing ... constructs the sense of who we are by a real engagement with the strangeness of the past. ... We are set free from the crippling imprisonment of what we can grasp and take for granted, the ultimate trivialising of our identity.[39]

That is, seeing tradition in terms of the complex history of the lived reception of divine revelation may also help to guard against a false belief that what we do and believe is part of an easily defined continuity of faith or practice.

An awareness of the complexity of the history of the Church – understood to mean the whole people of God – introduces us to quite a different sense of what it is to stand in the company of all the saints. Williams argues:

> Who I am as a Christian is something which, in theological terms, I could only answer fully on the impossible supposition that I could see and grasp how all other Christian lives had shaped mine, and more specifically, shaped it towards the likeness of Christ.[40]

---

39 Rowan Williams, *Why Study the Past? The Quest for the Historical Church* (London: Darton, Longman & Todd, 2005), p. 24.

40 Williams, *Why Study the Past?*, p. 27.

A deeper understanding of the richness of the Church's tradition arises out of a better understanding of the way in which the Church has struggled with similar questions of how they should respond to the gospel and live out their faith in the past. Consequently, to engage with the complexity of expressions of faith in the past is to take seriously the true Catholicity of the Church, whilst remaining aware also of its apostolicity, for it is to take seriously the important ecclesiological insight all Christians of the past contribute to the fullness of what it means to be Christian, and thus to the richness of the full being of the Church. An understanding of tradition which focuses only on particular aspects of the past will lose much of this richness, and ignore much of what has sustained living faith. *The Gift of Authority* affirms that, when we explore the ways in which our forebears experienced the living Word of God in their lives,

> There may be a rediscovery of elements that have been neglected ... There may also be a sifting of what has been received because some of the formulations of the Tradition are seen to be inadequate or even misleading in a new context.[41]

Gaining new perspectives on the complexity of tradition is a reminder of how our forebears struggled with questions, just as we do. And it is a reminder too that we may stand in the tradition of the Church even if – or precisely because – we ourselves come to different answers than did those of previous generations. In the fraught context of the later English Reformation, Hooker affirmed that 'the Church hath authority to establish that for an order at one time, which at another it may abolish, and in both do well'.[42] Writing of liturgical renewal, Elizabeth Smith suggests, 'Somewhere in this tension between

---

41 TGOA, § 25.
42 Hooker, *Ecclesiastical Laws*, V.viii.2.

innovation and continuity, between individuals' gifts and communities' needs, lies the fertile ground for growing new words, new visual images, and new body language to take Anglican worship into its next stage of its evolution.'[43] Finding the creative balance between continuity and innovation is part of the tradition which Anglicanism – and indeed the whole Church – inherits.

For us, as for Hooker, much of the discussion centres on the ordering of the ministry. In this context, a study of the early Church's discussions of women ministry is revealing as to the motive for excluding women from the ministry of preaching and baptizing. The *Didascalia Apostolorum* suggests that a major objection to having women in leadership is that the communities to which they preach were reluctant to accept the teaching authority of a woman. The arguments for the exclusion of women from the ordained ministry are shaped by the interests of preaching the gospel in a very different context to our own.[44] As Chadwick has commented, in antiquity, 'outsiders would mock the church if it had women priests of bishops. In the West of the twentieth century, outsiders mock the church because it has none'.[45] Sharing in the mission of the Church – accepting our 'fellowship in missionary duty', and the 1938 Doctrine Report put it – in which case may mean changing our practice, in order to stand firm with that tradition

---

43 Elizabeth J. Smith, 'Women, Word, and Worship: Changing the treasury of resources', in *Anglican Theological Review* 82 (2000), pp. 113–128, here p. 124.

44 For more detail, see Charlotte Methuen, 'Vidua–Presbytera–Episcopa: Women with Oversight in the Early Church,' in *Theology* 108 (2005), pp. 163–177; and cf. also eadem, 'Women with Oversight: Evidence from the Early Church' in James Rigney with Mark D. Chapman (eds), *Women as Bishops* (London: Mowbray 2008), pp. 72–92.

45 Chadwick, 'Ministry and Tradition', p. 18.

of proclamation. Similar observations can be made of the ministry of those living in committed relationships with people of their own gender, especially in countries where civic legislation has moved to accept those relationships, or even to recognize them as marriage. This is a very different situation from that envisaged by Paul or the authors of the Old Testament. Has the Church ever really had to deal with this question before? A study of statements against the practice of homosexuality suggests that they are directed at something rather different. The question is certainly complicated by the very different legal situations of gay people in much of the Western world compared to parts of Africa and Asia, but a simple appeal to the truth of a decontextualized text or to an acontextual understanding of the tradition of the Church is not a real answer.

Tradition and the Future

As we ask such questions, we are seeking to define the authority of, not only scripture, but also of tradition, and with the question of how and in response to which challenges tradition changes and grows. The question is not *whether* tradition changes and grows. It does. Every tradition – however old, however well established – had a beginning. Knowing about that beginning may help us to discern whether it still breathes life, whether it still is a means for passing on the living gospel. That means that we need an understanding of tradition which takes historical context seriously, which takes our own history seriously and which takes the history of the concept itself seriously.

To stand in the tradition of the Church, then, is to engage with a process of critical discernment. It is not simply about defining tradition to be those things which were done or which worked for earlier generations, but also about understanding it to encompass those things which may not have seemed to work then, but which might offer to us authentic ways of responding to the gospel. If our tradition is to be liberating and life-giving – if it is to be of the gospel – we need to be afraid of it, not to be afraid of understanding where what we believe and how we express those beliefs came from, how it has changed. In other words, we need to understand what has shaped what we do, why we began doing it, and to think about why we still do it. And in all of that, the tradition of the Church challenges us to live the gospel of Christ out of the past in the present and into the future.

3

The Authority of Reason?
The Importance of Being Liberal

MARK D. CHAPMAN

Liberal-minded Anglicans have not in general majored on utter depravity. Although the Thirty-nine Articles of Religion are not silent on the matter, and Article Nine is certainly somewhat forthright about original or birth sin, many have tended towards what is called there the 'vain talk' of the Pelagians, a heresy which allows for a modicum of goodness to be performed through the capacities of the human being. However, for many Christians, most of whom certainly wouldn't regard themselves as Pelagian, human reason displays something of the continuity with the original righteousness that was not completely demolished by the Fall. There are a lot of liberals who would certainly fall into this category. According to this view it is through their own capacities, especially through their faculty of Reason, that human beings can in some way do what God wants of them without the complete need for grace, whether common or particular. For those who are interested in Richard Hooker, the precise role of original sin in his thought is a major bone of contention. He has varied from being understood as what Basil Willey called a 'God-centred humanist',[1] to virtually a fully

---

1   Basil Willey, *The English Moralists* (London: Chatto and Windus, 1964), p. 102; Peter Lake, *Anglicans and Puritans? Presbyterian and English Conformist Thought from Whitgift to Hooker* (London: Unwin Hyman, 1988), pp. 150, 182.

fledged Calvinist,[2] and all stations in between.[3] In all this, reason has played a particularly prominent role.

There are many resonances between Hooker's thought and many of today's problems. This is hardly surprising since Hooker wrote his great multi-volume book on ecclesiastical polity in the context of the conflict provoked by the problem of how to decide on the issue of what to wear in church and whether the Book of Common Prayer was really a 'mass book full of abominations'.[4] The real problem was this: where did the authority come from on those matters which were not expressly ruled out by scripture? For Hooker, human beings had a rational faculty which could decide on such things, provided that they always acknowledged the primacy of scripture.[5] At least some of the debate over the rights and wrongs of homosexuality has been couched in terms of whether or not it is expressly ruled out in Scripture. But I don't want to go any further into Hooker's theology: I have no great desire today to enter the debate on the use of reason in the sixteenth century, nor to talk about threefold cords, and whether Hooker was really reformed or a proto-Laudian.

Instead I want to start looking at reason from the perspective of utter depravity. I have to admit that I have a fairly cultivated sense of original sin – it is probably something that comes with living in a theological college for sixteen years. Instead of

---

2 Nigel Atkinson, *Richard Hooker and the Authority of Scripture, Tradition and Reason: Reformed Theologian of the Church of England?* (Carlisle: Paternoster, 1997), ch. 1.

3 Nigel Voak, *Richard Hooker and Reformed Theology: A Study of Reason, Will and Grace*, (Oxford: Oxford University Press, 2003), ch. 3.

4 Walter Frere and C. E. Douglas, *Puritan Manifestoes: A Study of the Origin of the Puritan Revolt, with a Reprint of the 'Admonition to the Parliament', and Kindred Documents, 1572* (reprint, London: SPCK, 1954), p. 21.

5 See, for example, *Ecclesiastical Polity* I.xvi.5; I.xiv.2

beginning with the authority of reason I begin the authority of scripture, and with St Paul's simple statement: 'all have sinned and fall short of the glory of God' (Romans 3.23). For Paul, everything depends utterly on the grace of God. If I am a liberal I am not the sort of liberal who places a great deal of trust in human reason or natural law, which is as equally open to corruption and idolatry as any other human product. Like Luther I am inclined to see human reason as 'the devil's bride'. I would not want to share his terminology but I share some of his sentiment. He calls reason 'that pretty whore', who 'comes in and thinks she's wise'.[6] On its own, and as a source of doctrine, reason does not count for much.

And yet reason is still central to the Christian faith – but only when it draws on a serious theology of sin. So what I want to talk about in this lecture is a different kind of reason that is built on a recognition of the fallibility and frailty of all human constructions. It is what one could call a perpetual critical method that constantly subjects everything to scrutiny and testing – including those things that look most holy. Since I know I have sinned I am forced to be sceptical about all those things I think I believe and think are true. As a sinner I know I may be wrong. Of course they may be true – but they are always mediated through my shaky senses and perceptions. My judgement – like the judgement of everybody else – clouds everything I know or do. And it is this perception of sin that makes me a critical scrutineer of religion. It is this method that I choose to call liberal, which is an inadequate and misleading word – but what I am going to talk about is liberal in a very

---

6   Martin Luther's Last Sermon in Wittenberg (Second Sunday in Epiphany, 17 January 1546). *Dr. Martin Luthers Werke: Kritische Gesamtausgabe* (Weimar: Herman Boehlaus Nachfolger, 1914), vol. 51:126, line 7ff.

distinctive way. This, of course, will make me very unpopular in many parts of the Church – but I'm used to that.

Woolly Liberalism

Let me illustrate all this with an allusion to the secular world. When he was Home Secretary Charles Clarke faced criticisms that he was being too soft on terrorism and crime. In response he remarked with less than a perfect command of English grammar: 'I don't like liberals. I am not soft. I am neither woolly or liberal or a woolly liberal. I have never been a liberal in my life. I don't like liberal with a capital L or a small l.'[7] Being a soft woolly liberal is not considered one of the great twenty-first-century virtues, especially for a Home Secretary facing the perceived threat of ever-increasing levels of terrorism. And being a woolly liberal in religious matters is probably the greatest insult of all. Some work hard to avoid the accusation. For instance, Paul Avis, Secretary for Ecumenical Affairs for the Church of England, in arguing for the importance of the good liberal virtues of dialogue and openness, nevertheless stresses that what he means is not 'a woolly liberal sell-out' but 'quite the reverse'. He goes on:

> The Gospel, rather than the world, sets the agenda. Openness is an economy for the sake of mission. I do not overlook the need for a strong centre of identity in the Church, for clarity of belief as far as this is possible, for a message with a gospel cutting-edge.[8]

On this model, the world, while something that clearly has to be engaged with and listened to, is ultimately to be sliced through with a relatively clear set of beliefs which are

---

7   Reported in *The Independent* (3 September 2005).
8   Paul Avis, *A Church Drawing Near: Spirituality and Mission in a Post-Christian Culture* (London: Continuum, 2003), p. 35.

presumably quite distinct from those of the world. The world, it would seem, is opposed to the gospel.

This sort of language, even when stated in this benign and apparently unthreatening way, provides ammunition for the critics of religion. With its set of certainties and crusading zeal (admittedly somewhat moderated), Christianity is simply not capable of being self-critical liberal and tolerant of others. This means that it would be far better for religious people – together with their unwitting defenders who peddle the multiculturalist agenda – to own up to the real character of religion, which is about hatred of difference and promotion of utter certainty and absolute obedience. Writing in *The Observer* a few days before 9/11, the noisy philosopher, A. C. Grayling, claimed that

> It is a woolly liberal hope that all religions can be viewed as worshipping the same deity; … but this is a nonsense … the motivation for Christianity's hundreds of years of crusades against Islam, pogroms against Jews, and inquisitions against heretics, was the desire to expunge heterodoxy and 'infidelity', or at least to effect forcible compliance with prevailing orthodoxy. Islam's various jihads and fatwahs had and have the same aim, and it spread half way around the world by conquest and the sword.[9]

There is no space here for liberal religion. Instead throughout history the true colours of all religion are revealed in their gruesome splendour.

At the same time, some less vitriolic critics of religion just do not see the point of being self-critical in religion. Indeed they see the decline of anything other than sectarian forms of religion with their absolute necessities as inevitable. Liberal religion might have served an important function in liberating

---

9   A. C. Grayling, 'Keep God out of Public Affairs' in *The Observer* (12 August 2001), at: http://observer.guardian.co.uk/comment/story/

those who had been brought up in authoritarian versions of religion, but it could hardly survive into the future. The sociologist, Steve Bruce writes that liberal religion was almost bound to decline since it was almost impossible to transmit it to the next generation.[10] The only sort of religion that can resist this process of decline, he maintains, is that which can command coercion – in other words, the religion of the sect or of an authoritarian Church.

Prophetic Liberalism

Those of us who have an interest in the survival of a self-critical form of Christianity into the future need to address these critiques, which is why I want to begin with the bold claim that a significant amount of woolly liberalism is necessary for the functioning of a healthy Christianity. This is something that needs to be re-asserted in the contemporary Church, particularly when there are so many who would like to confine Christianity solely to its more uncritical, dogmatic and sectarian forms. And I would contend that the reason for this is extraordinarily simple and uncontentious, even though it is a claim seldom made by liberals (as I suggested at the beginning): whatever else religion might be, it is a human practice open to all the distortions of human sin, which means it simply demands to be scrutinized and criticized. This is something that would be understood by the Hebrew prophets and virtually every reformer since. For the greater glory of God there is thus a responsibility to open up our practices and beliefs to critical scrutiny since they too are part of that sin in

---

0,,535543,00.html#article_continue (accessed 28 August 2009).

10 Steve Bruce, 'The Problems of a Liberal Religion', in Mark D. Chapman (ed.), *The Future of Liberal Theology* (Aldershot: Ashgate, 2002, pp. 221–41, here p. 233. See also, *Religion in the Modern World* (Oxford: Oxford University Press, 1996), pp. 85–91.

which all of us participate. Here, I think, is where a fairly strong dose of criticism becomes necessary for all Christians – and it is rooted in the doctrine of sin. Liberalism in this critical sense is consequently far more an attitude of mind than a church party, and it can even look prophetic.

Now, I would not want to belong to anything called a liberal party in the Church – I'm much too traditional in my religion. I am a good solid Anglo-Catholic who prays a lot and who is really quite conservative in much of his theology, but my disposition and attitude is liberal. I am a participating critic. For Anglo-Catholicism this is important – and not too difficult. After all, it doesn't take too much effort to reveal the ironies, hypocrisies and idolatries of Anglo-Catholicism. But at the same time the continued vitality of religion requires that it be practised, cherished and loved, and approached with reverence and awe. This means that the liberal will usually have a love/hate relationship with the religion that he or she professes.

Even Karl Barth, not usually regarded as a liberal theologian, understood this process. He likens the need for constant critical vigilance to a rather vertiginous walk along a mountain ridge:

> On the narrow ridge of rock one can only walk: if one attempts to stand still one will fall either to the right or to the left, but fall one must. There remains only to keep walking – an appalling performance for those who are not free from dizziness – looking from one side to the other, from positive to negative, and from negative to positive. Our task is to interpret the Yes by the No and the No by the Yes, without delaying for more than a moment in either a fixed yes or a fixed no.[11]

---

11 'The Word of God and the Task of Ministry', in *The Word of God and the Word of Man* (London: Hodder & Stoughton, 1928), pp. 206–7.

51

Liberalism is thus more an attitude of mind, a process of engagement with living religion, than a form of religion itself. This means – and here I am different from many who label themselves 'liberal' – that sectarian and dogmatic varieties of Christianity have a crucial place, even within the Church of England. These types can be persuasive and convincing and they will offer places where we find identity and coherence – but they need to be carefully circumscribed and scrutinized lest they become idols which define themselves as bounded systems over and against others. That was precisely what Barth was trying to do with the religion of his own upbringing. And that is where a critical liberal disposition comes in.

As a disposition and a way of engaging with religion, then, liberalism is not a church party like the others – those prepared to exercise criticism exist across the board. They have taken different sides in the ritualist controversies and matters of church and state. This is hardly surprising, since methodological scepticism and critical engagement do not necessarily favour a particular set of practices. Instead the liberal disposition will subject the diverse practices of all types of religion to critical assessment and appraisal. This means that there will be many different varieties of liberalism, as liberals subject the various types of religion to scrutiny. Indeed, almost from its inception, members of the Church of England from across its traditions have seen it as their job to ask the difficult questions about the religion they were professing. And in the last 150 years or so most Anglican 'liberals' have used the term as a description of a way of approaching their particular variety of the Anglican religion – there were 'liberal catholics' (a term pioneered by Charles Gore) and 'liberal evangelicals' (a movement associated with Vernon Storr) and even 'liberal' radicals. And it is also obviously true that there were also many illiberal practitioners of all these forms of religion.

Consequently, with that great liberal catholic, Alec Vidler, I would claim that 'in the economy of the Church there is a need for both types' of religion – 'the unreasonably confident and the astringently sceptical; both have their indispensable contribution to make to the mission and message of a church'.[12] And that is certainly true for me: as I have said, I am by nature a man with a sceptical turn of mind, and I am quite well aware that such an attitude is not likely to appeal to the majority. Nevertheless, I would want to contend that the 'unreasonably confident' need to have somebody to turn to who is happy to point to idolatry or to criticize any tendencies to latch onto voguish ideologies and prevalent moods. The 'perennial office of the liberal in the Church and in society', writes Vidler, 'is to be critical and astringently so ... He must be *impartial* in his criticism, which is to say that the formation of a liberal party in the Church is a double contradiction in terms. Liberals will always be in a minority. Their role is a subordinate, but a salutary, and antiseptic or aperient, one'.[13] This means that sometimes the principal liberal vocation will be to purge the constipated religion of the parties; at other times it will be to point to complexity and to obfuscate and to confuse. Some things just aren't that simple; and it can be important to challenge false simplicity. This may mean disclosing sillinesses and being far from certain, which is why liberalism often gets labelled 'woolly'. Consequently, whatever variety of religion one has (and for an Anglican that religion might be catholic, or evangelical, or charismatic, or middle of the road, and all points in between), it needs an injection of aperient and astringent liberalism if it is to function healthily. If that is the case then it might be said that there really is such

---

12   Alec Vidler, *Essays in Liberality* (London: SCM Press, 1957), p. 27.

13   *Essays in Liberality*, p. 25.

a thing as a liberal prophet – and that will often be a particularly uncomfortable position.[14]

The Broad Churchmen

There are many who will find this whole approach highly dubious. To be sceptical in religion and to adopt a critical stance will be to distrust the truth disclosed through revelation, and instead will lead to a vague universalism. This is what Cardinal Newman wrote late in his life about the failings of the liberalism which he had reacted against in the early years of the Oxford Movement:

> Liberalism in religion is the doctrine that there is no positive truth in religion, but that one creed is as good as another ... It is inconsistent with any recognition of any religion as *true*. It teaches that all are to be tolerated, for all are matters of opinion. Revealed religion is not a truth, but a sentiment or a taste; not an objective fact, not miraculous; and it is the right of each individual to make it say just what strikes his fancy. Devotion is not necessarily founded on faith. Men may go to Protestant Churches and to Catholic, may get good from both and belong to neither. They may fraternise together in spiritual thoughts and feelings, without having any views at all of doctrines in common, or seeing the need of them. Since, then, religion is so personal a peculiarity and so private a possession, we must of

---

14 In saying this I want to differentiate the sort of liberalism I have in mind from other forms of liberalism which have been more partisan and dogmatic in their expression. Many critics (including most obviously Karl Barth) have seen liberalism and liberal theology as little more than an apology for the inevitability of progress, which has obviously been shattered by so many of the cataclysmic events of the last hundred years. Herbert Spencer's words ring rather hollow: 'Progress is not an accident, but a necessity. Surely must evil and immorality disappear; surely must man become perfect' (Herbert Spencer, *Social Statics* (first edition, 1892) (London: Routledge, 1996), p. 32).

necessity ignore it in the intercourse of man with man. If a man puts on a new religion every morning, what is that to you? It is as impertinent to think about a man's religion as about his sources of income or his management of his family. Religion is in no sense the bond of society.[15]

In part, I think, Newman is accurate in his understanding of liberalism in religion. It is a way of approaching truth that does not confine it to the Church. This means that, according to Newman, it has no space for positive revelation, and consequently it is bound to be a private matter and to lose its social impact. For Newman faith requires far more – first a belief in the supernatural foundations of the Church and its revelation, and secondly, obedience to her teachings. But where Newman misrepresented liberals in religion is in his claim that they deny 'positive truth in religion'. What he failed to perceive is that liberalism is a second-order activity where the truth of revealed religion is tested as faith seeks understanding. For this to happen the religious system cannot contain the whole of the truth; at the very least – and this is surely at the heart of a doctrine of sin – it must point to the limited nature and fallibility of human perception and knowledge, even in religious matters.

Let me illustrate this by looking at some of Newman's contemporaries, who are sometimes labelled liberals, but who were more usually designated Broad Church. This was a term first used by A. P. Stanley in a sermon in 1847 where he claimed the Church of England was broad, rather than either High or Low Church. Later, in his famous essay 'Church

---

15 See Wilfrid Ward, *The Life of John Henry Cardinal Newman* (London: Longmans, 1913), 2 vols, vol. 2, p. 460.

Parties', published in the *Edinburgh Review* of 1853,[16] W. J. Conybeare used the term to designate a third party alongside evangelicals and Anglo-Catholics, although he recognized the difficulty of the label. Friends tended to use Moderate or Catholic and detractors called them Latitudinarian or indifferent. In many ways the Broad Churchmen adopted a straightforward and traditional form of Anglicanism, but they also saw the importance of engaging critically with that very tradition. Truth was regarded as resting beyond the confines of any worldly system, and all people had the God-given capacity to pursue this truth, unfettered by any absolutist claims of the past. Contrary to Newman's claim, there was positive truth in religion, but that truth was one and the same truth that could be also be found in the highest achievements of human beings through the centuries. Christianity was thus not *sui generis* but was part of a shared human quest for truth. Nevertheless, nothing could contain the whole of truth, which was ultimately to be found only with God.

For the Broad Churchmen, the Christian vocation was principally to be human, a vocation which itself required a discipline and method if it was to be successfully pursued. The call to education in the sense of cultivation of the higher instincts is in many ways the most characteristic feature of mid-Victorian religious life – and it is this aspect that shaped the Broad Church approach to Christianity more than anything else. The most important figure in this movement is undoubtedly Thomas Arnold (1795–1842), headmaster of Rugby from 1828 and the most influential educationalist of his generation. Christianity, he held, was the fundamental moral discipline required to approach life with a set of ideals and

---

16 New edition edited by Arthur Burns in 'Church Parties' in Stephen Taylor (ed.), *An Anglican Miscellany* (Church of England Record Society, vol. 7) (Woodbridge: Boydell, 1999), pp. 213–385.

with a mind cultivated by higher ends. In a famous letter to John Tucker, Arnold wrote:

> My object will be, if possible, to form Christian men, for Christian boys I can scarcely hope to make; I mean that, from the natural imperfect state of boyhood, they are not susceptible of Christian principles in their full development upon their practice, and I suspect that a low standard of morals in many respects must be tolerated amongst them, as it was on a larger scale in what I consider the boyhood of the human race.[17]

Education was about the formation of the Christian character which was able to think for itself. In this way the school would function as a microcosm of the great Christian task of the education of the human race.[18] In this task religion occupied a central place. Dean Stanley wrote about Thomas Arnold's understanding of religion, claiming that, for Arnold,

> religion – the relation of the soul to God – depends on our own moral and spiritual characters. [Arnold] made us understand that the only thing for which God supremely cares, the only thing that God supremely loves, is goodness – that the only thing which is supremely hateful to God is wickedness. All other things are useful, beautiful in their several ways. All forms, ordinances, means of instruction, means of amusement, have their place in our lives. But religion, the true religion of Jesus Christ, consists in that which makes us wiser and better, more truthful, more loving, more tender, more considerate, more pure. Therefore in his view, there was no place or time from which religion is shut out – there is no place or time where we cannot be serving God by serving our fellow creatures.[19]

---

17 A. P. Stanley, *The Life and Correspondence of Thomas Arnold* (London: John Murray, 1897), 2 vols, vol. 1, p. 71.

18 On this, David Newsome, *Godliness and Good Learning* (London: John Murray, 1961).

19 R. E. Prothero, *Life of Dean Stanley* (London: John Murray, 1893), 2 vols, vol. 2, p. 455.

For Arnold, then, religion was about the cultivation of a habit with which to approach the whole of life so that good was pursued and evil avoided. This meant that the Church was not to be understood as a distinctly religious society, but was instead 'a society for the purpose of making men like Christ, – earth like heaven, – the kingdoms of the world the kingdom of Christ.' The Church was something that should pervade everything and could never be regarded simply as 'an institution for religious instruction and religious worship'. This would rob it 'of its life and universality, making it an affair of the clergy, not of people – of preaching and ceremonies, not of living – of Sundays and synagogues, instead of all days and all places, houses, streets, towns and country'.[20] Arnold was working with a unified vision of nation and Church as part of an all-embracing whole, or what he called 'the "idea" of the Edward the Sixth Reformers'.[21]

Arnold, like Samuel Taylor Coleridge before him, regarded Christianity fundamentally as a life rather than a set of doctrines,[22] but a mature life which was disciplined by what Coleridge called 'manly energy'.[23] The cultivation of what to future generations might have been considered an effete and perhaps even effeminate form of manliness is well expressed by B. F. Westcott, the future bishop of Durham, and one of the greatest New Testament scholars of his generation. In 1849 he wrote to his future wife:

> You have often heard my views of life, yet hear them once again ... To live is not to be gay or idle or restless. Frivolity, inactivity, and aimlessness seem equally remote from the true

---

20 Stanley, *Life of Arnold*, Vol. 2, p. 13.
21 Stanley, *Life of Arnold*, Vol. 2, p. 12.
22 *Biographia Literaria* (1817), p. 212.
23 *Aids to Reflection*, aphorism XII.

idea of living. I should say that we live only so far as we cultivate all our faculties, and improve all our advantages for God's glory. The means of living then will be our own endowments, whether of talent or influence; the aim of living, the good of man; the motive of living, the love of God.[24]

For Westcott, as for Arnold, the conception of truth is not restricted to the Church – instead all faculties are to be improved for the glory of God.

Frederick Temple

A similar approach can be glimpsed in the work of Frederick Temple (1821–1902), headmaster of Rugby from 1850, who went on to become Archbishop of Canterbury. He contributed an essay entitled 'The Education of the World' to a collected volume published in February 1860 called *Essays and Reviews*.[25] This book of seven essays by men mainly with Oxford connections proved to be one of the most controversial books of theology published in the nineteenth century. Temple's essay itself was probably the least controversial. Basil Willey thought that 'it will stir no emotion in a modern reader save one of boredom'.[26] Nevertheless, it offers a good example of Broad Church theology. Temple's contribution was based on the supposed and rather far-fetched analogy between the education of the individual and the life of the human race. In both cases there were three stages: childhood corresponded to the period before our Lord's coming; youth and early manhood to our Lord's period on earth; and full manhood corresponded to the period which followed after Christianity

---

24 Arthur Westcott, *Life and Letters of Brooke Foss Westcott* (London: Macmillan, 1903), 2 vols, vol. 1, p. 145.

25 References to the tenth edition (London: Longmans, 1862).

26 Basil Willey, *More Nineteenth Century Studies: A Group of Honest Doubters* (Cambridge: Cambridge University Press, 1956), p. 141.

was young. Thus even before Christ, the history of the world was one of increasing maturity, although for Temple no stage can ever match the new stage initiated by Christ. He outlines four different aspects of human development. The Hebrews, he claims, 'may be said to have disciplined the human conscience, Rome the Human Will, Greece the reason and taste, Asia the spiritual imagination'.[27]

Human beings move on from the necessary rules of childhood (analogous to the Law of the Old Testament) to a situation where instead of mere obedience they begin to exercise their reason, even though they will constantly falter. Yet as they mature, so they increase in discipline, not by returning to a childish unthinking legalism, but rather to a discipline based on thinking things through. Criticism thereby becomes a religious duty as human beings examine what Temple calls the 'really valuable principles' underpinning their practical life. He writes:

> To learn toleration well and really, to let it become, not a philosophical tenet, but a practical principle, to join with real religiousness of life and character, it is absolutely necessary that it should break in upon the mind by slow and steady degrees, and that at every point its right to go further should be disputed, and so forced to logical proof ... the slowness of [the] progress [of such toleration] gives time to disentangle from dogmatism the really valuable principles and sentiments which have been mixed up and entwined in it, and to unite toleration, not with indifference and worldliness, but with spiritual truth and religiousness of life.[28]

Growing up is thus about disentangling the truth from its entrapment in dogmatism, and that requires a respectful and cautious liberal disposition.

---

27 *Essays and Reviews*, p. 23.
28 *Essays and Reviews*, pp. 55–6.

Temple claimed that even when applied to the Bible and the truths of the Christian faith this liberal method would not necessarily lead to despair. Indeed, the process of testing might make faith far more secure:

> The substance of the teaching which we derive from the Bible will not really be affected by anything of this sort. While its hold upon the minds of believers, and its power to stir the depths of the spirit of man, however much weakened at first, must be immeasurably strengthened in the end, by clearing away any blunders which may have been fastened on it by human interpretation.[29]

The goal of religion is thus to clear away the human blunders that have served to conceal the truth – in different language it is about freeing the Word of God from the words of men. This means that the study of the Bible can be no different in kind from any other earnest truth-seeking intellectual pursuit:

> Not only in the exercise of religious truth, but in all exercise of the intellectual powers, we have no right to stop short of any limit but that which nature, that is, the decree of the Creator, has imposed on us ... If we have made mistakes, careful study may teach us better. If we have quarrelled about works, the enlightenment of the understanding is the best means to show us our folly.[30]

To be liberal was to be an adult and to recognize that God had granted to us the powers of criticism, '[f]or,' Temple writes, 'we are now men, governed by principles, if governed at all, and cannot rely any longer on the impulses of youth or the discipline of childhood'.[31] Criticism was the sign of human

---

29 *Essays and Reviews*, p. 57.

30 *Essays and Reviews*, pp. 57–8.

31 *Essays and Reviews*, p. 58.

maturity and human beings ought to recognize that they could not return to some ironclad truth beyond the possibility of critique without at the same time returning to the naïvity of childhood.

In the controversies that followed the publication of *Essays and Reviews*, Temple wrote to his friend, A. C. Tait, Bishop of London (and Arnold's successor as headmaster of Rugby) to emphasize this point. The critical study of the Bible, he wrote,

> imperatively demands freedom for its conditions. To tell a man to study, and yet bid him, under heavy penalties, come to the same conclusions with those who have not studied, is to mock him. If the conclusions are prescribed, the study if precluded.
>
> Freedom plainly implies the widest possible toleration.[32]

Critical study, which is the mark of human maturity, forces tolerance on the Church; and without it ignorance would continue. Temple goes on:

> I know what can be said against a wide toleration. It may be said that it would issue in wild and extravagant speculations. So it would, in a few instances. But you know perfectly well that there is not the most distant chance of the great mass of sober Englishmen running into anything of the sort. If therefore you tolerate extreme opinions, their very existence in the Church is a guarantee that the moderate opinions are held from conviction, not from fear of consequences. But if you drive extreme men out of the ministry, the inevitable result is to poison the minds of the laity with the suspicion that the clergymen who remain teach what they do, not because they believe it, but because they fear the fate of their brethren.
>
> I for one joined in writing this book in the hope of breaking through that mischievous reticence which, go where I would, I perpetually found destroying the truthfulness of religion. I

---

32   25 February 1861, cited in William Benham, *Life of Archibald Campbell Tait* (London: Macmillan, 1891), 2 vols, here vol. I, p. 291.

wished to encourage men to speak out. I believed that many doubts and difficulties only lived because they were hunted into the dark, and would die in the light.

I believed that all opinions of the sort contained in the book would be better if tolerated and discussed, than if censured and maintained in secret. And though there was much error mixed up in these opinions, yet certainly not more than in what was allowed, and even encouraged. What can be a grosser superstition than the theory of literal inspiration? But because that has a regular footing it is to be treated as a good man's mistake, while the courage to speak the truth about the first chapter of the Book of Genesis is a wanton piece of wickedness. A wide toleration would in time set all these matters in their true relation; for if neology has strong defenders, certainly the commonly received opinions have no lack of able men to maintain them.[33]

For Temple, the quest for truth could not be restrained without dire consequences for intellectual honesty and for an intelligent ministry. This required a wide toleration, even of extremes, since only then would more moderate men begin to think issues through. Indeed without this approach the Church would be guilty of hypocrisy. This meant that the veils of secrecy and clerical control had to be removed, and investigation had to be carried out in the open.

Benjamin Jowett, Regius Professor of Greek at Oxford, and shortly afterwards Master of Balliol, whose essay in the volume, entitled 'On the Interpretation of Scripture',[34] was the longest and probably the most important, wrote to A. P. Stanley about the purpose of the book. The object of the essayists, he claimed, was to liberate the truth,

to say what we think freely within the limits of the Church of England ... We do not wish anything rash, or irritating to the

---

33 *Essays and Reviews*, p. 292.
34 In *Essays and Reviews*, pp. 399–527.

> public or the University, but we are determined not to submit to this abominable system of terrorism, which prevents the statement of the plainest facts, and makes true theology or theological education impossible.[35]

As so many of those who entered into the controversy noted, what was at issue was the nature of truth, and precisely how that truth was to be understood and circumscribed. The defenders of orthodoxy who restricted critical thought, Stanley held, were the real terrorists. Most churchmen, however, thought otherwise. For instance, Samuel Wilberforce, Bishop of Oxford, noted in the *Quarterly Review* that he could not see how the writers could 'with moral honesty maintain their posts as clergymen in the Established Church'.[36] A letter of censure from nearly all the English and Welsh bishops followed soon after publication.[37] Huge petitions were gathered from Evangelicals and Anglo-Catholics in a rare moment of common endeavour. A court case dragged on for a number of years, finishing in 1864 with relatively indecisive conclusions which did not silence the authors permanently.[38] Pusey, never prone to understatement, thought that the crisis provoked by *Essays and Reviews* and the failure of the courts to censure the writers was 'a struggle for the life and death of the Church of England'.[39] 'Without some combined effort to repudiate the Judgment,' he wrote to Wilberforce, 'the Church of England

---

35 E. Abbott and L. Campbell, *The Life and Letters of Benjamin Jowett* (1897), vol. 1, p. 275.

36 *Quarterly Review* (January, 1861), p. 302.

37 *Life of Tait*, vol. 1, pp. 282–3.

38 On this see Ieuan Ellis, *Seven against Christ: A Study of Essays and Reviews* (Leiden: Brill, 1980); and Josef L. Altholz, *Anatomy of a Controversy: The Debate over Essays and Reviews* (Aldershot: Scolar Press, 1994).

39 Pusey to Stanley, 23 February 1864, in H. P. Liddon, *The Life of E. B. Pusey* (London: Longmans, 1897), 4 vols, vol. 4, p. 63.

will be destroyed or will become the destroyer of souls.'[40] But the Church of England survived, and much of what the authors had written soon became acceptable even for clergy to hold. Temple himself was consecrated Bishop of Exeter amid controversy, but went on to become Archbishop of Canterbury with no objections except to his advanced age.

Conclusion

The point of this lengthy excursion into Victorian theology is not primarily to defend the Broad Churchmen. After all, theirs was often a rather elitist and nationalist understanding of Christianity, and many of them found the more aesthetic religion of their more catholic-minded contemporaries quite unacceptable. Instead I want to stress the role of critical thought in strengthening religion through testing: very few liberals ever sought to create a new form of religion. Instead virtually all tried to reinforce the credibility of the brand of religion through which they experienced the power and beauty of God. And this will be as equally true for Anglo-Catholics as anybody else. There were very few who tried to remove the essentially irrational core which was the foundation of religious practice and the Christian life and to replace it with some kind of rationalist faith. As Temple shows, the contention of most Broad Churchmen was that religion is strengthened through the activity of critical thought. Or, in the words of St Paul: 'When I was a child, I spoke like a child, I thought like a child, I reasoned like a child; when I became a man, I gave up childish ways' (1 Cor. 13.11).

Of course some people who start to think things through will jettison their faith, but for many others the opposite will prove true: faith will be strengthened though testing. The irrational heart of faith in God will rest on more secure foundations, but

---

40   Pusey to Wilberforce, 13 February 1864, in Liddon, vol. 4, p. 52.

the detritus of the centuries will begin to be cleared away, even though we might well place new detritus in the way. This process of testing will undoubtedly shake certainties – and things may even become woolly – but that is often a good thing. After all, this side of eternity we 'see in a mirror dimly' (1 Cor. 13.12). Things that are dim are usually fuzzy and unclear, which is why critical thought ends up so woolly. As Samuel Wilberforce said of *Essays and Reviews*: trying to understand what the authors meant was like 'grasping at a nebulosity or seizing upon a sepia'.[41] But it seems to me that a degree of nebulosity in religious matters is an inevitable part of the human condition. This means that those of a critical liberal disposition can carry on being religious; they can carry on doing those strange religious things which allow them to glimpse something of the glory of God. But as they do so, humility, reticence and caution will be their typical demeanour. As with so many of the mystics, the light will often be shrouded in mist, and the colour of religion may well be the colour of an English sky – a shade of grey that can last for months at a time. Maybe that is why there have been so many great English mystics.

Those with a critical liberal disposition live in a symbiotic but often uneasy relationship with others who share their faith. But they need to be tolerated lest people forget to ask the questions and lose sight of their fallibility. In the wake of *Essays and Reviews* Bishop Tait expressed his own sense of exasperation.

> The folly of the publication of *Essays and Reviews*, [has] ... so effectually frightened the clergy that I think there is scarcely a Bishop on the Bench, ... that is not useless for the purpose of

---

41 Cited in Standish Meacham, *Lord Bishop: The Life of Samuel Wilberforce: 1805–1873* (Cambridge: Harvard University Press, 1970), p. 221.

preventing the widespread alienation of intelligent men ... Meanwhile I feel my own vocation clear, greatly as I sympathise with the Evangelicals, not to allow them to tyrannise over the Broad Churchmen; and to resist that tendency which is at present strong in them to coalesce with the High Church party for the mere purpose of exterminating those against whom the cry is now loudest ... What is wanted is a deeply religious liberal party, and almost all who might have formed it have, in the alarm, deserted ... The great evil is that the liberals are deficient in religion, and the religious are deficient in liberality. Let us pray for an outpouring of the very Spirit of Truth.[42]

It is not clear to me that things have changed. Deeply religious liberals are still needed – and they exist across the parties of the Church of England and beyond. It is the responsibility of all those who approach Christianity with that sense of critical enquiry and testing to return to their churches of whatever hue and to prod and disturb and assist in the process of human maturing – so that all Christians can begin to put away childish things. That is why I am a liberal Catholic and not just a liberal. And it is why I want to prod and disturb those fellow catholics with whom I most disagree – and sometimes people are prepared to listen to what I might have to say. Those with this critical disposition in their different churches and parties will not necessarily have an easy ride – they may even disturb the certainties of those churches as they challenge them to think things through. But they will also assist those churches in their quest to see God face to face, and to recognize the distortions that emerge as we gaze on God through the scaly eyes of human sin, distortions that often masquerade as divine certainty. Criticism is a scary thing.

There is thus something absolutely central in a form of critical liberalism in the Church as a kind of para-church

---

42   *Life of Tait*, vol. 1, p. 325.

movement, living off the wider religious body, yet helping that body to grow freely, to develop and to mature. There is, however, little point in being critically liberal in the Church unless one is also deeply religious. And if we are serious about that, we have to face up to the fact that often the attempt to be a religious liberal who is not deficient in religion will be a struggle and it may well meet with conflict. But it remains vital for the future of a vibrant and intellectually credible Christianity, which seeks for God among the cluttered world of human certainties. This means, as Alec Vidler wrote:

> The liberal vocation, faithfully exercised, is not only humbling but also reconciling. It has the effect of showing that no party or school of thought or phase of orthodoxy is ever as right as its protagonists are inclined to suppose, and that men, including Christian men, have much more in common both of frailty and strength, both of falsehood and truth, than the makers of systems and sects acknowledge.[43]

This task is an enormous responsibility but it is also exciting and motivating. Indeed it is nothing short of what Dr Pusey called 'a struggle for the life and death of the Church of England'. And I hope that Affirming Catholicism exists, not as another party, but as a way of promoting that thorn-in-the-flesh sort of self-criticism which all religion requires.

---

43   Vidler, *Essays in Liberality*, p. 26.

4

Theology and the Renewal of the Church

ANDREW DAVISON

Since its foundation, *Affirming Catholicism* has been concerned with the renewal of the Church. In this chapter I want to consider how theology has contributed to this goal in the past, and how it might do so again. My argument will be that we need more theology in our Church and more church in our theology. I will begin, quite deliberately, with a story to cheer us, namely the fruitful relationship between theology and ecumenism. After that, we will have to face a gloomier scene and the spectacle of Anglican Catholicism playing down the Church. As a further irony, we find a collapse in confidence in both church and theology at the end of a century that rediscovered the importance of the Church in theology. Reconnecting with this tradition might renew our vigour and purpose. The final section will look at Cardinal Kasper's call for 'a new Oxford Movement'. Like the nineteenth-century movement, this would have to be a renewal of theology in the Church and of the Church by theology.

Ecumenism

The twentieth century was a marvel of ecumenism. At its beginning, a Roman Catholic could not pray the Lord's Prayer alongside a Methodist, and prejudice against Catholics was deeply engrained in English culture. The century closed with the Archbishop of Canterbury kneeling beside the Pope in the millennium year to open the Holy Door at St Paul's without the Walls.

For all these gains, ecumenism has now entered a new and difficult period, especially between our Church and the Roman Catholic Church. This is the much-discussed 'ecumenical winter'. To comfort ourselves, we often remember the resilience of local ecumenism. Small-scale joint projects and joint services continue. We have come to take them for granted. Alongside this I want to place academic theology as another significant and enduring triumph of ecumenism – and one which is not always given its due. Theology provides fertile soil in which ecumenism can grow and flourish.

Today, theology can no longer be insular. Although it is rightly carried out within particular traditions, these traditions are no longer sealed off. Although many theologians work out of a deep loyalty to a particular Church, one of their gifts to their churches is to forge links beyond their bounds. Which Protestant scholar of patristics could ignore the work of Rowan Williams or Henry Chadwick? Which Anglican liturgical scholar could ignore the work of the Roman Catholics Aidan Kavanagh and Robert Taft, or the Lutheran Gordon Lathrop? Which Roman Catholic scholar of philosophical theology would ignore John Milbank or Sarah Coakley? The most significant and fruitful theologians of the past century have exercised their influence across the traditions. All theology was changed by Karl Barth. Every theologian must respond to the challenges laid down by liberation theology, which was very largely Roman Catholic in origin.

The ecumenical nature of academic theology can be illustrated quite simply by looking at our British theology faculties. Anglicans, Roman Catholics and Protestants work side by side. This is the case in Cambridge and London, in Exeter and Oxford. We may take this for granted, but it appears somewhat remarkable viewed from outside the United

Kingdom, especially from a Continental European perspective. While I was a student at Westcott House, and before Josef Ratzinger was made Pope, I had the good fortune of a private audience. As we sat in the Holy Office drinking tea, two questions exercised the cardinal: the health of the Queen Mother and how it could be that theologians from the Church of England and the Roman Catholic Church taught side by side in Cambridge. I was able to give the cheerful answer that it worked very well. How, he asked, did they agree on what to teach in ecclesiology? The less cheerful answer was that the doctrine of the Church featured very little. His surprise, I imagine, was born of the confessional demarcation of theological faculties in Continental Europe. We are liable to forget the gift for ecumenism presented by our system. Theological exchange across church divisions is the day-to-day life of our university departments.

The Church in Theology

I have begun with the picture of theology as an unsung driving force for ecumenism. I have done so because it is a fairly uncomplicated success story. It is something for us to be pleased about. Such stories are all the more necessary at the moment, as the Church of England can be a gloomy place to be. Anglo-Catholics, in particular, are not in great heart, whether they style themselves as 'traditionalists' or 'progressives'. In recent years we have dedicated so much attention to problems in the Church that we have come to see the Church itself as a problem. This applies across our divisions, although in different ways. 'Traditionalist' Anglo-Catholics relate to the Church to which they belong, the Church of England, as something to be resisted, resented and cajoled. Liberal Anglo-Catholics are no better. In their disapproval of an institution seen as repressive and sluggish, they have turned away from

71

the Church, in practice if not in theory. They have defined themselves in terms of identity politics and not in terms of baptism; they have expressed themselves in secular arguments, not theological ones.[1]

Our attitude towards the Church as Anglo-Catholics – by turns aloof and disdainful – is all the more ironic given that we stand at the end of a century when theology rediscovered the importance of the Church. Theologians from many different perspectives came to appreciate the significance of the Church as a theological topic. They saw its indispensable place within the overall framework of doctrine, and within the saving purposes of God in particular. In twentieth-century theology there was what I would like to call a 'Return to the Church'. If we could appreciate this, and catch something of the vitality of these ideas, it would go some way towards raising our mood and restoring our confidence.

Let me turn first to Pauline scholarship. The last few decades have seen a significant reappraisal of Paul's theology.[2] As part of this, Biblical theologians have returned to the idea that 'incorporation into Christ' holds a central place in Paul's thought.[3] In particular, the concept of being 'in Christ' is

---

1   Evangelicals, we might suppose, have never had sufficient room in their theology and imagination for the Church. It is an irony that their distance from the Church has been replicated, in various ways, by Anglo-Catholics. It is a further irony that evangelicals at present are turning their back on something they *did* once value highly: doctrinal theology.

2   The shifts discussed below can be situated within the wider sweep of the 'New Perspective on Paul' associated with James Dunn, N. T. Wright, E. P. Sanders, Krister Stendahl and others. A summary of the wider concerns of these scholars can be found in James D. G. Dunn, *The New Perspective on Paul* (Grand Rapids: Eerdmans, 2007).

3   In the words of James Dunn, the 'study of participation in Christ leads more directly into the rest of Paul's theology than justification [does]' (James D. G. Dunn, *The Theology of Paul the Apostle* (Grand

central.[4] Several important trends in interpretation follow on from this. There is a renewed sense that Paul sees salvation as communal and ecclesial rather than simply individual.[5] Justification is being rethought in terms of incorporation into the Body of Christ[6] and even in terms of deification, thanks to

---

Rapids, MI: Eerdmans, 1997), p. 395). The sense that incorporation was central for Paul was popular at the beginning of the twentieth century, due to the work of Adolf Deissmann, Wilhelm Bousset and Albert Schweitzer. This approach fell out of favour, in part because the idea was overplayed but also because it was inimical and incomprehensible to the individualist modern mind. See: Dunn, *Theology of Paul*, p. 391 and E. P. Sanders, *Paul and Palestinian Judaism: A Comparison of Patterns of Religion* (London: SCM Press, 1977), p. 453 and Morna Hooker, *Paul* (Oxford: Oneworld, 2003), p. 84. The importance of incorporation and participation has now again resurfaced.

4   Again in the words of James Dunn, 'Paul's "in Christ" language is much more pervasive in his writings than his talk of "God's righteousness"' (*Theology of Paul*, p. 319). According to Morna Hooker, this is 'Paul's favourite expression', *Paul*, p. 84. The theme has been important in the writings of N. T. Wright. For a popular introduction see *Paul: Fresh Perspectives* (London: SPCK, 2005), p. 46. For a sustained scholarly discussion, see 'ΧΡΙΣΤΟΣ as "Messiah" In Paul: Philemon 6', in *The Climax of the Covenant: Christ and the Law in Pauline Theology* (Edinburgh: T&T Clark, 1991), pp. 41–55. See also E. P. Sanders, *Paul and Palestinian Judaism*, pp. 455–6.

5   See, for instance, E. P. Sanders, *Paul* (Oxford: Oxford University Press, 1991); J. A. Ziesler, *Pauline Christianity* (Oxford: Oxford University Press, 1990), p. 72; Jouette M. Bassler, *Navigating Paul: An Introduction to Key Theological Concepts* (Louisville, KY: Westminster John Knox Press, 2007), especially chapter 4: James Dunn, *Theology of Paul*, p. 411; Morna Hooker, *Paul*, p. 86; and Michael J. Gorman, *Apostle of the Crucified Lord: A Theological Introduction to Paul and His Letters* (Grand Rapids, MI: Eerdmans, 2004), pp. 126–7.

6   Sanders provided the important insight that being 'in Christ' is central to Paul's understanding of the atonement, which must

some Finnnish Lutherans[7]. Similarly, scholars are emphasizing the extent to which Paul's ethics are communal ethics.[8] By Aristotle's definition, to draw attention to the communal-ethical in Paul is to say that his theology is inescapably *political*. Sure enough, there has been a thoroughly surprising flowering of interest in Paul among secular political theorists, especially on the left (albeit on their own terms). He has featured prominently in the writings of Alain Badiou, Giorgio Agamben, and Slavoj Žižek.[9]

---

therefore be seen as more than sacrificial. See *Paul and Palestinian Judaism*, pp. 465–68.

7   For an overview, see Jonathan Linman, 'Martin Luther: "Little Christs for the World": Faith and Sacraments as Means to *Theosis*' in Michael J. Christensen and Jeffery A. Wittung, *Partakers of the Divine Nature: The History and Development of Deification in the Christian Traditions* (Madison, NJ: Fairleigh Dickinson University Press, 2007). For more detailed studies, see Veli-Matti Kärkkäinen, *One with God: Salvation as Deification and Justification* (Collegeville, MN: Liturgical Press, 2005); and Tuomo Mannermaa, *Christ Present in Faith: Luther's View of Justification* (Minneapolis, MN: Augsburg Fortress, 2005). For the texts of the dialogues between the Finnish Lutheran and Russian Orthodox theologians which initiated this work, see Hannu Kamppuri (ed.), *Dialogue Between Neighbours: The Theological Conversations between the Evangelical–Lutheran Church or Finland and the Russian Orthodox Church 1970–1986* (Helsinki: Luther–Agricola Society, 1986).

8   James Dunn, *Theology of Paul*, p. 411; E. P. Sanders, *Paul and Palestinian Judaism*, pp. 454–5, and elsewhere; Richard B. Hays, *The Moral Vision of the New Testament: Community, Cross, New Creation* (Edinburgh: T&T Clark, 1997), pp. 196–7; Michael J. Gorman, *Apostle of the Crucified Lord*, p. 128; J. Louis Martyn, *Theological Issues in the Letters of Paul* (London: Continuum International, 2005), p. 261. The theme is developed across several of N. T. Wright's books.

9   Alain Badiou, *Saint Paul: The Foundation of Universalism* (Stanford, CA: Stanford University Press), 2003; Giorgio Agamben, *The Time That Remains: A Commentary on the Letter to the Romans* (Stanford, CA: Stanford University Press), 2006; Slavoj Žižek, *The Puppet and*

Doctrinal theology has also seen a reawakening to the Church. In the first half of the twentieth century there was a renewal of interest in the Church as the Body of Christ. From an Anglican perspective, we need only think of John Robinson's *The Body: A Study in Pauline Theology* (1952).[10] In other traditions, this was preceded by Sergei Bulgakov's *The Orthodox Church* (1935)[11] and *The Bride of the Lamb* (1945),[12] Henri de Lubac's *Catholicisme: Les Aspects Sociaux du Dogme* (1938),[13] and *Corpus Mysticum: L'Eucharistie et l'Église au Moyen Âge* (1944),[14] and the encyclical *Mystici Corporis* by Pius XII (1943). The significance of Robinson's book must be stressed. He returned the image of the body its proper place as an acknowledged centrepiece of the Pauline literature. 'The concept of the body', he wrote, 'forms the keystone of Paul's theology'.[15] As a consequence, for Paul the Church embodies the gospel. The link between her identity as the Body of Christ and her practice is never far from his mind. Not least, the Church embodies the reconciliation at the heart of the gospel and a new sort of fellowship. In this, it is the sign and the agent of God's promise for the whole universe. In the words of Robinson,

The hope of Christians is nothing less than that the complete fullness of God which already resides in Christ should in Him

---

the Dwarf: The Perverse Core of Christianity (Cambridge: MA: MIT Press. 2003).

10   London: SCM Press.

11   English translation: Crestwood, NY: St Vladimir's Seminary Press, 1989.

12   English translation: Grand Rapids, MI. William Eerdmans, 2001.

13   Translated as *Catholicism: Christ and the Common Destiny of Man* (San Francisco: Ignatius Press, 1988).

14   Translated as Corpus *Mysticum: The Eucharist and the Church in the Middle Ages* (London: SCM Press, 2006).

15   *The Body*, p. 9.

become theirs. This can never be true of isolated Christians, but in the 'fullgrown man', in the new corporeity which is His body, 'the measure of the stature of the fullness of Christ' is theirs to attain (Eph. 4.13) – for the Father's decree is that the Divine fullness should dwell in Him, not simply as an individual but σωματικῶς [bodily].[16]

In the twentieth century we were reintroduced to the idea that the Church takes forward the work of Christ. We find this idea in twentieth century Anglican writing: in Eric Mascall, for instance in *Christ, the Christian and the Church: A Study of the Incarnation and its Consequences*[17] and in Michael Ramsey's *The Gospel and the Catholic Church*.[18] It is also prominent in the figures I have already mentioned, Henri de Lubac, and Sergei Bulgakov. The latter puts it particularly forcefully: 'The Church is the work of the Incarnation of Christ, it is the Incarnation itself'.[19]

This presents us with a stirring vision of the Church and her mission. She is the Body of Christ and the agent of the Incarnation. There is more, however, even than this. The Church not only advances the work of salvation as a means but also as part of the goal. Salvation is a communal union with God through Christ in his Body. Salvation is 'Church-shaped'.[20] Again, there are practical, even political, reper-

---

16 *The Body*, p. 69. The allusion with σωματικῶς is to Colossians 2.9, 'for in him the whole fullness of deity dwells *bodily*'.

17 London: Longmans, Green and Co, 1946.

18 London: Longmans, Green and Co, 1936.

19 *The Orthodox Church*, p. 2. The relation of the Church to the Incarnation has sometimes been pressed to such extremes as to suggest a form of hypostatic union between Christ and his Ecclesial Body. This has been resisted by others, including Pius XII in *Mystici Corporis Christi*, §54.

20 For a fuller discussion of this point in the light of the Pauline literature, see my forthcoming book on ecclesiology and Fresh

cussions. It means that the form of our life here and now matters. As de Lubac has it, expressing a thoroughly Pauline instinct, the Church is 'the true universal community in embryo'.[21]

De Lubac's prose has a fervour that we might not expect to find in English Anglican writing, but his themes are there in Ramsey and Mascall, who was an important conduit for the ideas of Bulgakov into the English-speaking theological world. Even the subtitle of Mascall's *Christ, the Christian and the Church* is suggestive: 'A Study of the Incarnation and its Consequences'. He spells this out in the introduction:

> I have attempted in this book to exhibit the Incarnation of the Son of God as the foundation and the unifying principle of the life and thought of both the individual Christian and the Church of which he is a member.... that incorporation into Christ is incorporation into the Church, since the Church is in its essence simply the human nature of Christ made appropriable by men, that all the thought, prayer and activity of Christians, in so far

---

Expressions in the Church of England considered from the perspective of the place of mediation in theology.

21   The phrase is John Milbank's summary of de Lubac's theology, *The Suspended Middle*, p. 2. The bracing and poetic writings of the French Jesuit Henri de Lubac are emerging as some of the more important works of the twentieth century. This renders all the more tragic the attenuation that marks the end of his life, after papal censure for modernism. For a brief introduction to his work, see the chapter on de Lubac in Fergus Kerr, *Twentieth-Century Theologians* (Oxford: Wiley Blackwell, 2006) and John Milbank, *The Suspended Middle: Henri De Lubac and the Debate Concerning the Supernatural* (London: SCM Press, 2005). For a lengthier introduction to his thought see Rudolf Voderholzer: *Meet Henri de Lubac: His Life and Work* (San Francisco: Ignatius Press, 2008); David Grumett, *De Lubac: A Guide for the Perplexed* (London: Continuum, 2007); and Hans Urs von Balthasar, *The Theology of Henri De Lubac* (San Francisco: Ignatius, 1992).

> as it is brought within the sphere of redemption, is the act of
> Christ himself in and through the Church which is his Body –
> these are the ideas that I have tried to expound.[22]

In the twentieth century theology regained a vision of the
Church in its glory, its dignity and its responsibility. To return
to this – simply to pick up these books and to read them again
– would revive confidence, renew the Church and inspire us to
hope and action.

The note of action, in particular, is an important one. To be
presented with a vision of the Church such as that in de
Lubac's *The Splendour of the Church* it to be both inspired and
disheartened. We will be reminded that parishes up and down
the country present us with communities both reconciled and
reconciling. We will also see how far we have to go. On this
theme, we would do well to supplement such rousing literature
with the commentary of a more critical figure such as Terry
Eagleton. In recent years his works have circled round
religious and even ecclesial themes. In *After Theory*,[23] and most
recently in *Reason, Faith, and Revolution*,[24] he defends the
Christian theological tradition as greater and more serious than
the philosophies and cultural theory of our own time. Once
they were the flag-bearers for politics, and even for revolution.
Now, according to Eagleton, they are largely bankrupt,
politically and ethically.[25] Even more insistently, Jesus emerges

---

22 *Christ, the Christian and the Church*, p. v.
23 Harmondsworth: Penguin, 2004.
24 New Haven, NJ: Yale University Press, 2009.
25 Christians who persist in judging Christian theology at the bar of
    post-structuralist philosophy would do well to read this eminent
    theorist's evaluation of contemporary philosophy and cultural
    theory.

as the hero in Eagleton's writing[26] and the voices of the various Dominicans who have influenced him, such as Herbert McCabe, are never far from the surface.

Almost alone in Western culture, Eagleton writes, the Christian tradition cares about the bodies of the poor and sick as well as of the rich and healthy. Nor are we transfixed by the naïve optimism of someone like Richard Dawkins.[27] For Eagleton, however, our theology is disproved because the life of the Church so rarely lives up to it. A Church worthy of its own traditions would be a remarkable thing – indeed, it would be a revolutionary thing. As it stands, for Eagleton, 'Religion has wrought untold misery in human affairs. For the most part, it has been a squalid tale of bigotry, superstition, wishful thinking, and oppressive ideology.'[28] Both de Lubac (and others like him) and Eagleton hold us to high standards in the way our communities embody the gospel. The former thinks that it can be achieved, and sometimes has. The latter thinks that it is too good to be true. We need to read both.

So far, this survey has taken in Orthodox, Roman Catholic and Anglo-Catholic sources. A new Church and communitarian focus is also emerging in the evangelical world. There is a marked shift away from an individualistic approach to Christianity and 'one's personal relationship with God'. It is the most noticeable where it is most necessary: in the evangelicalism of the United States. Here there have been substantial realignments of late. Environmental concerns were an important tipping point, with younger evangelicals no longer content with the scorn for science shown by older

---

26 Continuing this theme, he chose the Gospels as his contribution to the Verso series of revolutionary texts in 2007.

27 A recurrent theme in *Reason, Faith, and Revolution*.

28 These are the opening words of *Religion, Faith, and Revolution*, which is one of the most literate, learned and amusing attacks upon the New Atheists so far written.

leaders, nor with their apocalyptic desire to 'bring on the rapture'. We see it in the new prominence of 'left evangelicals' such as Jim Wallis and Stanley Hauerwas. We have seen something like it in the United Kingdom with the creation of *Fulcrum* and the unease of many Anglican evangelicals with the position taken by *Reform* and *Anglican Mainstream*.

A New Oxford Movement

Our focus so far has been on the twentieth century. The Church of England had its most decisive 'Return to the Church' with the Oxford Movement in the century before. It is this anniversary we are celebrating today.

As part of the recent Lambeth Conference, Cardinal Kasper[29] was invited to produce some 'Roman Catholic reflections on the Anglican Communion'.[30] More particularly, the Archbishop of Canterbury asked him to respond to the question 'what kind of Anglicanism do you want?'

Kasper began by stressing the significant affection in which our church is held by the Roman Catholic Church. I get the impression that these were heart-felt words:

> When the Second Vatican Council, in its Decree on Ecumenism, turned its attention to the 'many Communions (which) were separated from the Roman See' in the sixteenth century, it acknowledged that 'among those in which Catholic traditions and institutions in part continue to exist, the Anglican Communion occupies a special place' (*Unitatis redintegratio* §13).

Soon his speech turned to tensions in global Anglicanism, to the ordination of women, and to attitudes towards homosexuality and the exercise of authority. This left him pessimistic about the prospects for ecumenism in the future. If only, it

---

29   The head of the Pontifical Council for Christian Unity.
30   The date was 31 July 2009.

would seem, we would tow the line, reunion could be ours. The reply is obvious: here Rome is guilty of whatever is the opposite of crying wolf. For many years we have had the promise – the carrot – of full communion and the recognition of our orders always just around the corner. As a result, one more promise of unity, if only we would turn back on 'innovation', begins to ring hollow. That aside, here is Kasper's diagnosis:

> It now seems that full visible communion as the aim of our dialogue has receded further, and that our dialogue will have less ultimate goals and therefore will be altered in its character. While such a dialogue could still lead to good results, it would not be sustained by the dynamism which arises from the realistic possibility of the unity Christ asks of us, or the shared partaking of the one Lord's table, for which we so earnestly long.

He concludes by listing the 'many treasures' of the 'Anglican tradition', praising 'the beauty and eloquence of Anglican prayers', the 'fine scholarship of Anglican historians and theologians' and our 'significant and long-standing contributions ... to the ecumenical movement'. He is all the more aware of 'the greatness and remarkable depth of Christian culture' in our tradition because of the 'current problems and crises'.

It is, however, to his final words that I wish to draw attention:

> In that vein, I would like to return to the Archbishop's puzzling question what kind of Anglicanism I want. It occurs to me that at critical moments in the history of the Church of England and subsequently of the Anglican Communion, you have been able to retrieve the strength of the Church of the Fathers when that tradition was in jeopardy. The Caroline divines are an instance of that, and above all, I think of the Oxford Movement. Perhaps

in our own day it would be possible too, to think of a new Oxford Movement, a retrieval of riches which lay within your own household. This would be a re-reception, a fresh recourse to the Apostolic Tradition in a new situation. It would not mean a renouncing of your deep attentiveness to human challenges and struggles, your desire for human dignity and justice, your concern with the active role of all women and men in the Church. Rather, it would bring these concerns and the questions that arise from them more directly within the framework shaped by the Gospel and ancient common tradition in which our dialogue is grounded.

Cardinal Kasper called for a 'new Oxford Movement'. We may like the sound of this, but he cannot have one on his own terms, and neither can we. It is not inevitable that a new Oxford Movement would replicate contemporary Roman Catholicism within the Church of England. The churchmen and women who would produce such a revival are not obviously all thoroughgoing 'traditionalists'. And who knows, a new Oxford Movement might well be a Cambridge movement.

Neither Cardinal Kasper, nor we, can have a new Oxford Movement on our own terms. After all, Catholic Anglicanism flourished in the nineteenth century on nobody's terms. It was by no means 'tame'. It was deeply unsettling for all concerned. Its liturgical aspects were disturbing enough to provoke riots. More fundamental still, there were broadsides against corruption in Church polity, such as Keble's assize sermon, delivered 175 years ago. It also led to a quiet revolution in the work of the Church with the poor and in social justice.

Theological re-appropriations of the Tradition are deeply unsettling. We might think that a return to the Fathers would be received as an uncomplicatedly good thing by Anglicans, Protestants and Roman Catholics alike. In fact such 'returns' are often deeply provocative. Here it is useful to turn our attention to another Catholic renewal movement of great significance, that associated with the French *Ressourcement* theologians of the early and mid-twentieth century – Jean Daniélou, Yves Congar and Henri de Lubac (again), and alongside them, Marie-Dominique Chenu. They give us some sense of what 'another Oxford Movement' might look like, this time in Roman Catholic France. Again, it was not greeted with open arms. This has been explored at a popular level by Fergus Kerr in his *Twentieth Century Catholic Theologians*[31] and in a stimulating and careful analysis by Anna Williams in *The International Journal of Systematic Theology*.[32] Even the phrase by which we most often know their movement today, *nouvelle théologie*, was coined as a term of abuse.

At the end of the nineteenth century, Roman Catholic theology was static. The assumption was that the truth of the Christian faith had been codified for all time in the Neo-Scholastic system and that this was complete. This having been done, there was really no need to study earlier theological texts. The words of the Fathers had been drained of what they might contribute to this static, eternal and complete system. Compared to Neo-Scholasticism, the Fathers were immature, not quite there.

We can therefore imagine how disruptive it was for a group of academic priests to come along and claim that it is important to read the whole of the Tradition.[33] Not only that,

---

31 Oxford: Blackwell, 2007.

32 'The Future of the Past: The Contemporary Significance of the *Nouvelle Théologie*', in *International Journal of Systematic Theology*, 7(4). 2005, pp. 347–61.

33 In the words of Anna Williams, 'If the nouvelle théologie was not new inasmuch as it engaged neglected theologies of the past, it was new in its concern to revive interest in these at a time when they were thought to have become obsolete, and to do so in a way that not only made them the object of historical inquiry, but proposed

they began to publish these texts, with French translations, in the edition *Sources Chrétiennes*. To suggest that we look again at the Fathers was to suggest that there might be something incomplete about the timeless theological system that was supposed to have it all wrapped up.[34] This was deeply disruptive. For his part, Chenu weighed in on the role of Thomas Aquinas, whose work was taken as the basis for the Neo-Scholastic synthesis. For Chenu, Aquinas was principally out to think theologically about the problems of his day, rather than to produce the monolithic system into which his work had been turned.[35]

These *Ressourcement* figures were dangerous because they brought history to the foreground. The dry static picture, what Balthasar called *sawdust scholasticism*,[36] entertained only a limited sense of history: theological history led up to the post-

---

them as a quarry for constructive theology... The most immediate challenge of the *nouvelle théologie* was simply that it stirred up interest in the Christian past by making the rich array of older theology available, notably through the inauguration of *Sources chrétiennes'* ('The Future of the Past', pp. 349–50).

34 The early twentieth century was a time for disabusing us of our confidence in complete systems. In physics, the edifice of classical mechanics was already unravelling, since it was unable to model black-body radiation and could not account for phenomena such as the photo-electric effect. It was to be replaced, or supplemented, by quantum mechanics. In mathematics, Gödel's Incompleteness Theorems spelt the end of attempts at completeness exemplified by the work of David Hilbert, and of Bertrand Russell and Alfred North Whitehead.

35 For the history of this, see Anna Williams, 'The Future of the Past', p. 354; and Fergus Kerr, *Twentieth Century Catholic Theologians*, pp. 17–33. This was further argued by others such as Josef Pieper. In particular, see his *Guide to Thomas Aquinas* (San Francisco, CA: Ignatius Press, 1986), pp. 157–60.

36 The phrase is attributed to Balthasar by Fergus Kerr, *Twentieth Century Catholic Theologians*, p. 131.

Aquinas synthesis and then stopped abruptly. These Frenchmen suggested that everything could benefit from some historical perspective, even Aquinas. Worst still, they opened up the possibility that what came after might be less a matter of perfection than a matter of petrifaction. *Nouvelle théologie* renewed the Church by reminding it that theology is a living, breathing, debating, developing entity – as is the Church herself. This was not welcome at the time. If a cardinal had been praying for a new Oxford Movement in France, this is not what he would have wished for in advance.

The consequence of any return to the past that is worthy of the name 'Catholic' is dynamism for the present: whether with the Oxford Movement, *nouvelle théologie* or anything yet to come.[37] The Frenchmen shook the theological establishment of the day; the Oxford Movement outraged the Church of England. At his reception into the Roman Catholic Church, John Henry Newman was distrusted by many of his new co-religionists as a modernizing threat, not least because of his ideas on the development of doctrine (nicely anticipating twentieth-century opposition to the French writers). Any return to the tradition which had the vigour and seriousness of the Oxford Movement or of the *Ressourcement* cannot simply be assumed to support the status quo. Today many of our most significant Anglican theologians equip the Church to face the present and the future out of the riches of the past. Just think

---

37 Anna Williams offers the following observation, drawing upon the work and experience of the nouvelle théologie: 'The purpose of engaging older theology is not to constrain the parameters of contemporary theological expression, but to inspire, to provoke theological imagination to new insight. Not only development and variegation within the ancient and medieval tradition is presupposed, but flowering beyond it as the very consequence of interaction with it, such that it becomes impossible to engage with it without its bearing new fruit' ('The Future of the Past', p. 351).

again of Sarah Coakley, or John Milbank and his associates in *Radical Orthodoxy*. They are Catholics but they are by no means simply chips off the Vatican block.

All of this is very close to what *Affirming Catholicism* is about. You want living theology for a living Church, moving forward not *in spite of* the past but *on the basis of* the past. You want to be radical in both senses of the word: as activists and as *rooted* in the faith delivered to the saints. As someone who shares the historic goals of *Affirming Catholicism*, let me therefore offer a little criticism. You need to do more to engage Anglican Catholics who take theology seriously. The Church of England is blessed with an abundance of such people – clergy and lay, academic theologians, academics in other disciplines and many others with little formal education in theology. They are open minded and catholic leaning. *Affirming Catholicism* should appeal to people like this, to people who want to be theologically grounded and who find in those theological roots a call to action. The truth is, by and large, they are not involved with your society. They think that *Affirming Catholicism* has lost its theological nerve. They worry that it advances its arguments on the basis of liberal, secular principles rather on the basis of theology. The fact that your web site had a blank space for its page on 'what we believe' gives a bad impression. Similarly, I, you, the people I am thinking of – we all take the same stand on the big questions that face us, but *Affirming Catholicism* has to be more than a pressure group on a couple of issues. It is clear that you have a new sense of purpose here. You are reconnecting with your initial task of helping the Church to discover what it means to be Catholic. I wish you well, as this is tremendously important work.

The Church of England lacks confidence. It will return when we start taking the Christian faith seriously, and especially what it teaches about the Church. This would help to renew the Church. Christians cannot pass on or defend the faith unless they understand it. The evangelistic and apologetic work of the Church is predominantly lay work. The focus should therefore be on teaching and equipping the laity.

Since its inception, *Affirming Catholicism* has set itself the task of teaching Christian theology. The polemical issues are important, but the basics of the Catholic faith are more important still. The People of God need to understand what it means to be sons and daughters of the Church, and to take their place in the work of theology. Their role, in the words of Eric Mascall, is to

> take [their] tiny share, from [their] place in the Mystical Body, in the great task of rendering explicit the revelation committed to the Body by the Head with whom it is united. For, while the process of revelation attained its completion in the manifestation in human flesh of him who is, simply and finally, Prophet, Priest and King ... the displaying of all that is involved in that revelation is one of the great works of the Holy Spirit in the Mystical Body.[38]

---

38   *Christ, The Christian, and the Church*, p. 241.

5

Radical Anglicanism:
A Vision for the Future

JOSEPH P. CASSIDY

It is not an easy time to be an Anglican. For not a few times in the past few years, it has been more tempting to scream than to try, yet again, to figure out why it is still worth being an Anglican.

I should begin by saying that, by 'radical' Anglicanism, I mean something at the root of Anglicanism that is worth a huge commitment. So I use the term 'radical' in two ways: in terms of getting at the root or heart of it all and also in terms of a radical commitment to what *is* at the heart of it all.

So my question is: Is Anglicanism really an excellent way of being a Christian? Is it conducive to living the gospel or is it an obstacle? Or is it both? Does it lead to a real kind of holiness that the Church needs? Would any of us these days encourage someone to become or to remain an Anglican as a particularly excellent way of following Christ?

One of the things that is sometimes said to hold us back from promoting ourselves, which is to say from promoting our particular gifts, is our belief in provisionality: Anglicans have made much of the fact that they do not see Anglicanism as the paradigm for the whole Church, that they could imagine a re-united Church evolving that would require some quite signifi-cant changes in how *we* do church. That said, I do not entirely buy Stephen Sykes's idea that Anglican self-deprecation is the cause of much of this, and that this self-deprecation stems from the deeply ingrained cultural habit of self-denigration on the part of the English educated elite.[1] As a Canadian who has lived in the UK for close to 20 years, it has taken me a long time to realize that the English have an exquisite ability to *seem* self-deprecating *and* to put you in your place at the same time. Just watch a so-called cultivated English man or woman make a complaint: after a litany of self-deprecating apologies for even bothering to bother you, which softens you up and gets you smiling and feeling good about yourself, he or she slips in the matter of his or her complaint, and you find yourself wanting to agree, wanting to please. That's not self-deprecation; that's a finely honed killer instinct, where the prey dies smiling, but dies nonetheless. And I still get caught every time. It means complaints take longer than they need to, but the strategy works.

So provisionality may not be fully explained by reference to self-deprecation or self-denigration – at least not entirely. As many others have said, perhaps we simply need to agree on essentials: so long as we're united on essentials, united even on a small subset of the really essential, then we can be fairly relaxed about the non-essentials and so allow everything else to be provisional. But even that feels like a bit of a stretch these days, when we patently cannot agree on *what* the essentials are. And, as Stephen Sykes again has said, it is difficult to pin down any such fundamentals.[2]

---

1 Stephen W. Sykes, '*Odi et Amo*: Loving and Hating Anglicanism', in M. L. Dutton and P. T. Grey (eds), *One Lord, One Faith, One Baptism: Studies in Christian Ecclesiality and Ecumenism in Honor of J. Robert Wright* (Grand Rapids: Eerdmans, 2006), p. 195. As quoted in Paul Avis, *The Identity of Anglicanism: Essentials of Anglican Ecclesiology* (London: T&T Clark, 2007), p. 5.

2 See, for instance, Sykes, 'The Fundamentals of Christianity', in Stephen Sykes and John Booty (eds), *The Study of Anglicanism* (London: SPCK, 1988).

So should we even talk of Radical Anglicanism when we are faced with such differences within Anglicanism? Can we talk of Radical Anglicanism without privileging some particular and exclusive subset of Anglicanism?

I want to offer two approaches that may help us to imagine how we can identify something at the core, something that encourages Anglicans to remain Anglican these days, something that may even give Anglicans permission to feel some measure of confidence. One approach is to think of Anglican disagreements in terms of the way that ecumenism has developed. Another is to compare Anglicanism's position within the Church in terms of differences among religious orders within the Roman Catholic Church.

Ecumenical Insights

One of the more important things to realize about Anglicanism is that it is not a denomination. Rather it is a church of denominations, in the plural. A famous irony of Anglicanism is that Anglicans are often more open to other denominations, to other churches, than they are to other flavours of Anglicans.

The key shift in ecumenism in the last few decades, or so I have gleaned in part from Paul Avis,[3] is that expectations have shifted away from seeing reunification as a 'return to a united past' to seeing the goal as 'a form of unity that respects, indeed that expects, diversity'. The shift has been in appreciating the gospel's universality not in terms of a single way of being church for all time in all places, but in terms of the gospel's way of coming alive at all times and in all places. The universality of the gospel is precisely its universal applicability, its universal relevance, its universal challenge, its promise of grace in all times and in all places. And this is more than

---

3   Avis, *The Identity of Anglicanism.*

inculturation, at least as the term is often used or misused to describe how things are culturally adapted or translated. Rather, it is a type of universality that can coexist with some radical, even incommensurable, local differences, differences perhaps as radical, as Avis says, as those found in the four Gospels, or as radical as the differences between Peter and Paul, or as radical as the various apostolic churches as they first emerged.

For a long time, many of us thought that Church history evinced a trajectory towards catholic order (after all, we saw clear traces of it already in the New Testament itself); we thought that the true Church was unfolding providentially, under the sure influence of grace, as it coped with becoming larger, as it coped with the challenges of staying together as key theological arguments emerged. It was becoming clearer; a structure was coalescing. But the Church obviously did not remain united. And the result, the ecclesial reality, is a *series* of churches, of denominations, each emphasizing different facets of the gospel. Ecumenism today, arguably when it is at its best, does not want even to imagine a united Church without these different facets, without these different emphases – even if they are in tension with each other. Rather, the ecumenical movement is espousing recognition of each other as legitimate and as legitimately different – at least as a first step.

Ecumenism is not espousing relativism here: ecumenists anticipate that some of the distinctiveness will involve rival, conflicting truth claims, but without mutual excommunications.

So that's my first point, or rather that's Paul Avis's first point. If ecumenism is onto something by inviting and celebrating diversity and distinctiveness, then perhaps Anglicanism, with its own internal denominations, ought to be doing so as well. More than that, perhaps Anglicanism has *always* been doing this, though not always with a happy heart.

Of course, there's something about 'distinctiveness in unity' that is at the heart of it all. Our central insight into the Trinitarian nature of God suggests as much – or frankly demands as much. At the same time, arguments within a family are bound to be more painful than arguments outside. So adopting an ecumenical model for Anglicanism is not easy.

Now, this is neither earth-shattering nor very original, but that does not take anything away from the importance for Anglicanism of 'distinctiveness in unity' nor from the claim that this makes being an Anglican an excellent way of being a Christian. It is an openness not just to the anonymous other out-there-somewhere, but to the familiar, irksome other who is right next door, or even in the same family. It is a commitment to being the sort of Church that invites diversity, that does not insist on uniformity, that enables and permits strong disagreement, dare one say even on fundamentals, without anathematizing one another. It is a Church that welcomes profound and costly conversation, not just a parroting of the same old stuff amongst familiar friends who all think the same way. This may sound like a liberal, pluralist model, but it need not be: rather it is the model of a Church that expects the conversation to be getting somewhere over the longer term, that believes truth can and will emerge without using sticks, that stays together despite important differences because the truth will not emerge without the conversation. Indeed, a large part of the truth *is* engaging in the conversation, because that is where we actually experience the Holy Spirit working in those with whom we disagree. So we have common ground not so much at the level of our agreements, but at the level of attending to what God is enabling in us all.

Religious Orders

I'd like to expand this first model further by considering a different model -- religious orders. I could make the points I want to make by referring to Anglican religious communities, but I can speak a bit more knowingly about Roman Catholic religious orders, having been in one for half of my adult life.

Each religious order in the Roman Catholic Church has its own charism; and the charism stems from the founder or foundress of the order. It is quite personal in that sense: and so each order has a different personality. Each charism is a particular, perhaps even an exaggerated, take on one aspect of the gospel for the sake of the whole gospel. Thus the Capuchins, or Friars Minor, stress being lesser or minor, a Christ-like kenotic humility that opens them up to experiencing the privilege of serving the other. The Dominican charism emphasizes contemplation of the scriptures in order to proclaim the gospel with appropriate care and integrity. The Jesuit charism is radical availability, the freedom to be willingly sent on a mission anywhere in the world to serve the gospel – as seen in the Jesuit fourth vow, which is based on the mission of the second person of the Trinity's being sent by the Father. I could go on, order by order, but the key insight is that each of the historic Roman Catholic orders has a charism, the charism of its founder, which is a kind of practical wisdom, a path of holiness, which focuses on one or other aspects of living the gospel radically – it is not just a division of labour in the Church; it is rather an eschatological witness. You focus and exaggerate to draw attention, without thereby suggesting that the exaggerated model is a model for everyone, much as the vow of celibacy focuses attention on everyone's need to be single-hearted, without thereby being a model for everyone; or as the vow of poverty challenges our values and priorities without thereby ruling out private property.

So the religious orders 'contain' diversity: they provide a means of remaining in union with one another precisely by 'containing' or 'focusing' or 'legitimizing' this diversity. They provide a way for those who might otherwise leave the Church to live, what to their mind is, a less compromised life within an order *within* the Church (at least they may start out that way, until they discover their own weaknesses). But the thing is: the diversity is good. Jesuits do not dream of a day when all Dominicans will see the light and become Jesuits; in fact there are fairly strict rules against order-hopping.[4]

It is probably fair to say that most of the great theological differences that once characterized the Franciscans, Dominicans and Jesuits are behind us (differences on such diverse things as grace, tyrannicide or probabilism/probabiliarism), but such differences did exist, and there are still some dramatic differences in how the orders live their communal lives, how they understand their missions, how they follow Christ practically, which aspect of discipleship they emphasize. They do not argue about which is the best. Rather they have a sense that each is the best for some people, and that each could be the worst for other people.

Could it be that the most radical thing about Anglicanism is not the radical fervour of any one of its 'more correct' internal denominations, but the very fact of its having space for each of these denominations? Could it be that each internal Anglican denomination focuses on, and perhaps often exaggerates, some

---

4   Of course there are rivalries, as shown in that famous joke, where a Franciscan, a Dominican and a Jesuit were arguing about which order is the greatest. There's a huge thunderbolt, and a little piece of paper floats down. The three of them pick up the paper and read: 'All orders are equal.' It was signed, 'God, SJ'. (There may be *three* versions of the same joke, but one hopes not, as it would undermine the play on the Jesuits' well-known virtue of humility.)

aspect of the gospel, and that this could be a good thing – a way of reminding the whole Church of something truly vital? And could it be that such a limited focusing will always imply a distortion of some sort – a distortion that will become most obvious if one mistakenly claims that one particular way will and must fit all? But more on that later.

Holiness and Graciousness

There is a grace, a type of holiness, that can underpin this openness to diversity. All grace is concrete, and that's perhaps why it is often best communicated by narrative. Hence I want to change pace and recount two very simple, and admittedly personal, encounters with two brothers. These simple examples were chosen because the grace is very simple too, even if living according to such grace requires incredible heroism.

The first encounter was when I was a college student back in the early 70s. A number of us used to visit Benedict Vanier, a Trappist monk at Oka, just north of Montreal. Benedict happens to be Jean Vanier's brother. We used to bring a picnic lunch, and Chris Elliot, our theology lecturer, used also to insist that we bring the ham sandwiches we'd normally bring to a picnic. Now Trappists do not eat much at the best of times, but when they do eat, they are vegetarians. So we'd bring our ham sandwiches, offer one to Benedict, and he would eat it, smiling and complimenting whoever had made the sandwich. I am not sure whether Chris was doing this as a playful joke on Benedict; whether it was to enable Benedict to choose hospitality over regulations (which Benedict invariably did); or whether he did it to show *us* how hospitality trumped such rules. Whatever the motive, I have remembered the encounter for almost 40 years. I presume that Benedict was committed to his vegetarianism, but what an unusual commitment. How many vegetarians eat whatever is served them, without so much as a comment?

The simple point I want to make is that there was a graciousness about Benedict: he was able to accommodate our meat-eating without making a point of it. He did not abandon being a vegetarian even when he ate our sandwiches; not at all; he simply made us feel comfortable being meat-eaters. I have to say that, as older teenagers, our being meat-eaters was the least of our sins, but he did not require us to change to share a meal with him. His freedom around food-rules made us, however, ask important questions about our own freedom.

Moving the clock forward quite a few years, a few months ago I welcomed Benedict's brother Jean Vanier to St Chad's College, in Durham. This was the second time I'd met Jean Vanier in 35 years, but each time I have encountered Jean, I have noticed two things (similar to what I noticed in Benedict): one is a sense of his acceptance of me, even though I hardly live up to his example; and another is a sense of being called to integrity, without being made to feel guilty – a wonderful, if too rare, experience.

In Jean Vanier's case, I am tremendously inspired by his simplicity, by his joy, which enables him to be present to people of all sorts. I'm challenged by such simplicity of heart; I frankly want some of it myself. There is a sense that the authenticity of his life *is* a sort of judgement on mine; but rather than feeling accused I feel energized by recognizing something stirring in me that seems in sympathy with the good I see in Jean Vanier. He doesn't try to convert me. He is content to live with his lights, confident that the grace that causes and enables the good in his life is the same grace enabling me to do something equally good (but different) in mine – and to do so in God's own time. One could imagine that Jesus might have had a similar, though perhaps even more intense, effect on the people he met.

The point of recounting these two reminiscences is to suggest that this type of simple-but-real holiness you see in the Vanier brothers is exactly the sort of holiness that ought to characterize a radically gracious Anglicanism. It urges the question of whether there is a way of living with differences, of remaining in conversation, such that 'the other' feels at home? Is there a way of recognizing that 'something' stirring in me when I encounter the other on the other side of a vexing issue? Can we trust such 'stirring' and let it lead wherever it does lead, instead of demanding instant capitulation to my view? Can we engage with each other so that we do not allow our differences to prevent our sharing ham sandwiches? Or the Eucharist? Can we find some way of disagreeing with one another without trying to make each other feel guilty? Is there any way of appreciating that some of our differences emerge because we actually do emphasize and even exaggerate different but nonetheless real aspects of the gospel? Can we allow each other to do so without recrimination?

Radical Anglicanism

'Radical Anglicanism' can truly evince an authentic type of graciousness, but it can also, and all too easily, get confused with good manners. That was one of the gentle criticisms made of one of Paul Avis's most recent books, but I think Avis got it exactly right: there is an Anglican knack, an Anglican genius, for holding things together in diversity – and not just for the sake of expedience. It is more than a knack, of course; for this sort of graciousness is real holiness. And this sort of graciousness ought to be appreciated as cutting to the very heart of the gospel, because it turns on a profound belief in the priority of grace. We did not cause our faith; we were called; and what's more, we were called while we were still sinners. That same priority informs a Catholic understanding of the sacraments, and it ought also to inform the way Anglican

Christians relate to one another. We do not use sticks (or Bibles or mitres) to beat each other up because God works by gracious invitation. God knows what God is doing; and we should take the cue. The Anglican Communion needs jaw-dropping generosity – the kind seen in those who are profoundly committed to what they believe and yet do not make those who espouse something different feel any the less. How? By disagreeing, yes, but not by excluding or demonizing. We do not exclude, we cannot demonise, because we know in our bones that we are not more worthy.

Just as each religious order has a charism that focuses on one or a few aspects of the gospel and so distorts it by stretching the gospel a bit in one direction rather than in another, so too, if graciousness is *the* Anglican charism, then focusing on graciousness will distort things too. Graciousness and breadth will seem like a lazy accommodation of contradictory views, a sloppy acceptance of incoherence, an indecisiveness or fudge that causes others to judge Anglican-ism as something impossible to pin-down. But this ought to be an expected and acceptable cost of having an intense focus on *one* aspect of the gospel rather than an equal focus on all the other aspects at the same. Thus our 'gracious' accommodation with those who do not recognize the orders of women means that we do truly lack something key in terms of coherent unity; but we tolerate this very real and incredibly frustrating lack as a way of witnessing to a more radical prior commitment to graciousness – a more fundamental touchstone, again reflecting the fundamental belief in the priority of grace. And this witness is made, with all its attendant difficulties, for the sake of the whole Church. Other churches will focus on other things – on permanence, on truth, on our redeemed fallenness – but Anglicans can focus particularly on the fact that we were *called* together, whether we always like it or not, because fundamentally there is only one Spirit, one Body of Christ.

Graciousness in the face of diversity is our humble way of letting God work on keeping Anglicans together.

In the end, graciousness ought to be synonymous with Anglicanism. It *is* an evangelical stance, inasmuch as it captures what is at the heart of the sinner's experience of undeservable forgiveness; and yet it is also quintessentially Catholic because divine antecedent grace or graciousness is the essence of the sacramental life, of the sacramental Church. We are gracious because we have been graced. And the more conscious we are of being graced, the more conscious we are of our own sin, and so the less likely we should be to exclude others. And even if we, as a Church, do not agree on what gratuity looks like when it ramifies through our theology, even if we do not agree on how gratuity and inclusiveness interlink and get expressed in our doctrines or morals, still we can insist that our polity, our practical communion, be defined by graciousness-in-action. If we do so, then we've struck the kind of radicalness that is worth looking for, the kind of radical graciousness that is well worth committing to, the kind that gives God some proper credit for keeping Anglicans around a shared table.

But this sort of Radical Anglicanism is costly. How do we live a more gracious, welcoming type of Christian life in a Church that may itself be less and less welcoming of diversity? This is the old challenge of how to be tolerant of the intolerant, of how to be critical of intolerance without being seen as superior or as intolerant ourselves.

Perhaps the only sufficient answer is to trust what we experience when we encounter the Vaniers of this world. Perhaps we need to rediscover the holiness of hospitality, of profound graciousness, and the humility that makes these possible in the first place. The scriptural bases are already there: preserve unity in humility by 'putting on the mind of Christ Jesus' (Phil. 2.5) or 'bear with one another charitably, in

99

complete selflessness, gentleness and patience' (Eph. 4.2): but we need to see and be pulled by the compelling beauty behind these tags. After all, God bears with us. We need to keep on being graciously inclusive, by including those who are currently outside or feel on the fringe, as well as by including those who want to define the boundaries more exclusively. Being gracious does not mean backing down when there are threats to inclusiveness. No, the challenge is to stand up with honest, disarmingly gentle, non-violent graciousness, even at the cost of some coherence.

All of this means being very strategic at times; it may mean accepting further division while insisting on continued mutual recognition by newer, more tightly defined 'denominations' within Anglicanism: achieving such mutual recognition will require not just graciousness but also some deft political insight. Should the Communion, for instance, absolutely rule out the possibility of recognizing the Anglican Church of North America or other emerging groups (as painful as that might be)? But graciousness would require that any recognition of these new groups be conditional on their agreeing to re-enter into some admittedly imperfect communion with ECUSA (again the differentiation of newly emerging religious orders can be a clue to how this could occur). The key thing is that this sort of insistence on a gracious arrangement should be required as the Anglican way, though it should also be regarded as provisional, as a less-than-satisfactory way-station on the way to reconciliation. This is perhaps the proper context for discussing Anglicanism's provisionality: the concessions made in the name of graciousness are assented to as ways of keeping the larger, longer unitive conversation going until the differences are either overcome or recognized as legitimate.

To conclude, our communion needs the new, more generous insights into diversity that mark modern ecumenism – we ought especially to learn from that movement because it has been so much a part of recent Anglican history. We also need the permission felt by the traditional religious orders to distinguish themselves from others: while remaining in the Church, they tried to live the gospel radically, but they did so in different ways, in ways that stretched the gospel in certain (non-universalizable) directions rather than others. There could be some wisdom there. But if we want to recognize and enable any such diversity, then we'll need to embrace the gracious holiness that we find when we encounter truly holy women and men. We need not apologize for accepting this divine grace: there is a beauty to breath-taking magnanimity, to huge-heartedness, to a humble commitment to costly catholic universality. For, without patient, forbearing, humble, expectant holiness, Anglicans will be reduced to fighting; and if there are winners and losers, then we are all losers.

6

Catholicity and the Future of Anglicanism

MARK D. CHAPMAN

Introduction

In this chapter I will address some very simple and closely
related questions, which do not necessarily have simple
answers: firstly, 'What does it mean for the Church of England
to be catholic?' Secondly, when Anglicans recite the creeds
and acknowledge their faith in one, holy, catholic and
apostolic Church, what are they doing? Finally, what sort of
catholicity does the Anglican Communion embrace? To
answer these questions I will compare Anglicanism with the
dominant model of catholicity adopted by the Roman Catholic
Church. However, I will begin with a brief historical digression
drawn from the early history of ecumenism. The great Dr
Pusey, who was undisputed leader of the Anglo-Catholics
following Newman's departure to Rome in 1845, changed the
title of the final volume of his three-volume series of *Eirenica*
following the First Vatican Council. The question which had
formed the title for the first edition, *Is Healthful Reunion
Impossible?,*[1] was changed in 1876 to *Healthful Reunion as
Conceived Possible Before the Vatican Council.* His labours to find a
consonance between the teachings of the Church of England
and the Roman Catholic Church, which had occupied him for

---

1   *Is Healthful Reunion Impossible? The Second Letter to the Very Rev. J. H.
    Newman DD* (Oxford: Parker and London: Rivingtons, 1870);
    second edition *Healthful Reunion as Conceived Possible before the Vatican
    Council* (1876).

much of the 1860s, were scuppered by the declaration of infallibility in 1870. Whatever sort of catholicity the two churches might have appeared to share before the Vatican Council was shown to be no longer remotely tenable. After the Council Pusey wrote to John Henry Newman: 'I have done what I could, and now have done with controversy and Eirenica.'[2]

Although the public response in England to the declaration of infallibility was more muted than that following the creation of an English Roman Catholic hierarchy in 1850, and did not result in widespread cries of 'no-popery', the future of ecumenism nevertheless looked bleak after the Council.[3] Indeed to some it seemed that the Council had functioned as a vindication of the traditional hostile English attitude to Rome. As Odo Russell, unofficial representative for the British Government in Rome, wrote to Lord Granville, the Foreign Secretary, shortly after the declaration:

> The independence of the Roman Catholic hierarchy has thus been destroyed and the supreme absolutism of Rome has at last

---

2   Pusey to Newman, 26 August 1870, in Henry P. Liddon, *Life of Pusey*, 4 vols (London: Longmans, 1897), vol. iv, p. 193. On Pusey's ecumenism, see my essays, 'Pusey, Newman, and the end of a "healthful Reunion": The Second and Third Volumes of Pusey's *Eirenicon*', in *Zeitschrift für neuere Theologiegeschichte/Journal for the History of Modern Theology* 15:2 (2008), pp. 208–31; and 'A Catholicism of the Word and a Catholicism of Devotion: Pusey, Newman and the first *Eirenicon*' in *Zeitschrift für neuere Theologiegeschichte/Journal for the History of Modern Theology* 14:2 (2007), pp. 167–90.

3   Josef L. Altholz, 'The Vatican Decrees Controversy, 1874–1875', in *The Catholic Historical Review* 57 (1972), pp. 593–605.

been obtained, established and dogmatized for which the Papacy has contended for more than a thousand years.[4]

However, to some, the declaration of infallibility was not necessarily bad news for the Church of England. Indeed, the irrationality of the doctrine provided a welcome fillip for the future of more rational churches – such as the Church of England – more able to come to terms with the modern world. Thus, according to Christopher Wordsworth, Bishop of Lincoln, who responded to the Council in 1870, the Church of England offered a refuge for those who might be led into complete infidelity following the victory of Ultramontanism. Unlike Rome, he claimed, the Church of England exhibited a

> religious system, rational, Scriptural, and primitive, recognising and expanding all the faculties of men and supplying all his needs, conducive to the progress of literature, science and art, and ministerial to the peace of households and the welfare of society.[5]

Anglican reason was thus pitted against the irrationality of Rome. Given that Wordsworth had given the prestigious Hulsean Lectures in 1848 under the title, *Babylon; or, the Question Examined, Is the Church of Rome the Babylon of the Apocalypse?,*[6] it is no surprise that he held out little hope for

---

4   Russell to Granville, 18 July 1870, in N. Blakiston (ed.), *The Roman Question: Extracts from the Despatches of Odo Russell from Rome, 1858– 1870* (London: Chapman and Hall, 1962), p. 459; cited in Robert Fitzsimons, 'The Church of England and the First Vatican Council' in *Journal of Religious History* 27 (2003), pp. 29–46, p. 29.

5   *The Guardian* (29 June 1870), p. 764. On Wordsworth and the Council see Fitzsimmons, 'The Church of England and the First Vatican Council', esp. pp. 32–3.

6   Originally published as *Is the Church of Rome the Babylon of the Book of Revelation?* (London: Rivington, 1850).

union with the Roman Catholic Church. All in all, there seemed to be very little room left for inter-church conversations following the Council, something which was demonstrated even more conclusively by Leo XIII's declaration of Anglican orders as null and void in 1896.[7]

Ecumenical debate has obviously moved a long way since the 1860s and '70s. The tone and the mood have changed significantly. In general, Anglican bishops no longer denounce the Pope as the Antichrist. In general, the anti-Catholicism of the past is no longer acceptable. Similarly the triumphalism of pre-Vatican II Roman Catholicism has given way to the 'change of heart' announced in the Decree on Ecumenism (*Unitatis Redintegratio*) of 1964.[8] The Spirit, it claimed, could use the other churches and ecclesial communities as 'means of salvation which derive from the very fullness of grace and truth entrusted to the Catholic Church'.[9] The Anglican Roman Catholic International Commission, which was initiated at the 1966 meeting between Michael Ramsey and Paul VI, has been one of the most fruitful ecumenical discussions emerging from the implementation of *Unitatis Redintegratio*.[10] The first Commission produced reports on Eucharist, Ministry and two on Authority which were drawn together into the lengthy Final

---

7 18 September 1896 at: http://www.papalencyclicals.net/Leo13/ l13curae.htm

8 'Decree on Ecumenism', in Walter M. Abbott SJ (ed.), *The Documents of Vatican II* (London: Chapman, 1966), pp. 341–66, here p. 351 (§7).

9 *Documents*, p. 346.

10 Pope Paul VI and the Archbishop of Canterbury (Michael Ramsey), 'The Common Declaration' (1966), in Hill and Yarnold (eds), *Anglicans and Roman Catholics*, pp. 10–11. On the history of the Anglican–Roman Catholic dialogue see Mary Reath, *Rome and Canterbury: The Elusive Search for Unity* (Lanham, MD: Rowman and Littlefield, 2007).

Report of 1982. There was a real desire on the part of the Roman Catholic representatives to move on as a 'pilgrim church'. The report claimed, for instance, that 'contemporary discussions of conciliarity and primacy in both communions indicate that we are not dealing with positions destined to remain static'.[11] The mood in which the discussions were undertaken was one of openness, humility and trust. This report was optimistic, claiming to have reached what was called a 'substantial' unity.[12]

In many ways ARCIC proved to be one of the high points of ecumenical dialogue, moving beyond the polemics of the past. Shortly before the report was published Pope John Paul II acknowledged this, describing the method as going

> behind the habit and thought and expression born and nourished in enmity and controversy to scrutinise together the great common treasure, to clothe it in a language at once traditional and expressive of the insights of an age which no longer glorifies in strife but seeks to come together in listening to the quiet voice of the Spirit.[13]

At the same time, however, despite this progress and spirit of generosity between the Communions, the issue of papal primacy proved one of the major stumbling blocks. While there were significant agreements on ministry and the Eucharist (although obviously *Apostolicae Curae* remains a major stumbling block), the question of authority – particularly of the relationships between different forms of conciliarism and

---

11   'Authority II', §33 (page numbers in 'ARCIC I: The Final Report' in Hill and Yarnold (eds), *Anglicans and Roman Catholics*, pp. 12–76), here p. 75.

12   'Preface', p. 13.

13   Pope John Paul II, Castelgondolfo, 4 September 1980, cited in Hill and Yarnold (eds), *Anglicans and Roman Catholics*, p. 96.

universal primacy – was very different. The history of Petrine primacy in both Communions was too sensitive a topic to allow for easy reconciliation. Very different models of catholicity were still at work. As the ARCIC Final Report noted, '[r]elations between our two communions in the past have not encouraged reflection by Anglicans on the positive significance of the Roman primacy in the life of the universal Church'.[14] Before discussing the ARCIC documents, however, it is necessary to outline the particularities of Anglican history, which help to explain the contested nature of catholicity. As Yves Congar observed in what remains one of the few sympathetic Roman Catholic discussions of Anglicanism:

> There is no other Christian communion which is so difficult to understand apart from its history as Anglicanism; the prime characteristic of its theology is to share in this relatively unique inseparability from the march of national history and of the general movement of ideas within the nation.[15]

Imperial Sovereignty and Catholicity

The issue of catholicity was highlighted by the break with Rome in the 1530s.[16] This was simply because at its beginnings the rationale and purpose of the Church of England were explained not doctrinally, as was the case with most of the other churches of the Reformation, but principally in terms of the rejection of Roman authority. It was not merely that Rome

---

14 'Authority II', §13, p. 66.

15 Yves Congar, *Dialogue Between Christians* (London: Chapman, 1964), p. 249. See also Aidan Nichols OP, *The Panther and the Hind* (Edinburgh: T&T Clark, 1993).

16 On this see J. Robert Wright, 'Anglicans and the Papacy', in Peter J. McCord, *A Pope for All Christians* (London: SPCK, 1976), pp. 176–212.

had strayed from the truth, but rather – and more importantly – no prince or potentate, ecclesiastical or temporal, had any right whatsoever to interfere in the spiritual or temporal affairs of a sovereign state. This even found expression in the earliest English-language liturgy, Thomas Cranmer's Litany of 1544. This was a simplified form of its Latin predecessors designed to be read in procession in parish churches and produced in the context of a war against France.[17] It implored the Good Lord to deliver us 'from the tyranny of the Bishop of Rome and all his detestable enormities'. While this phrase was removed from the Prayer Book in 1559, it nevertheless exemplifies something of the thrust of the English Reformation: the identity of the English Church was established on the basis of hostility towards the authority of the papacy.

Although it has been the subject of much historical debate, it is undeniable that a theory of 'imperial' sovereignty was one of the key aspects of the religious changes in England in the reign of Henry VIII.[18] In his momentous preamble to the Act in Restraint of Appeals of 1533, for instance, Henry's chief minister and vicegerent in spirituals, Thomas Cromwell

> manifestly declared and expressed, that this realm of England is an Empire, and so hath been accepted in this world, governed by one supreme head and king, having the dignity and royal estate of the imperial crown of the same, unto whom a body politic, compact of all sorts and degrees of people, divided in terms and by names of spiritualty and temporalty, be bounden and owe to bear, next to God, a natural and humble obedience.

---

17 Charles C. Hefling and Cynthia L. Shattuck (eds), *The Oxford Guide to the Book of Common Prayer: a Worldwide Survey* (New York: Oxford University Press, 2006), p. 23.

18 G. R. Elton, *England under the Tudors* (Third Edition, London: Routledge, 1991), pp. 160–8; W. Ullmann, 'This realm of England is an empire', *Journal of Ecclesiastical History*, 30 (1979), pp. 175–203.

Church affairs like testaments, tithes, and dispensations from canon law – which were necessary if one needed a marriage annulled – were to be 'finally and definitively adjudged and determined, within the king's jurisdiction and not elsewhere'.[19] Church and state alike were thus placed under the sole authority of the Crown, with no foreign potentate allowed any say whatsoever in English affairs. In the religious sphere this was quickly enshrined in the Thirty-nine Articles of Religion as Article 37 on Civil Magistrates: 'The Bishop of Rome hath no jurisdiction in this realm of England'.[20] This meant that the particular or national Church had authority in Controversies of Faith (Article 20) and ceremonies (Article 34).

Even though there were important links and discussions with continental protestant churches, the principal focus of the English Reformation was on the character and nature of the independent Church of England rather than its international or confessional allegiances.[21] However, although the doctrinal settlement of Edward VI's reign was clearly strongly reformed, the Church that emerged from the Reformation continued to see itself as in some sense catholic and universal. It expressed its doctrine in terms of the three creeds (the Nicene, Apostles' and Athanasian), which meant that it regarded itself as part of the one catholic and apostolic Church. The title page of the Book of Common Prayer expresses something of this sense of catholicity: the book contains the orders and rites 'of the Church according to the use of the Church of England'. The

---

19   24 Henry VIII. c. 12. 3 S. R. 427.
20   Article 36 of Cranmer's original Forty-two articles of 1553.
21   On this, see Anthony Milton, *Catholic and Reformed: the Roman and Protestant Churches in English Protestant Thought, 1600-1640* (Cambridge: Cambridge University Press, 1995); and *The British Delegation and the Synod of Dort (1618–19)* (Woodbridge: Boydell, 2005). See also Patrick Collinson, *The Religion of the Protestants: The Church in English Society, 1559–1625* (Oxford: Clarendon Press, 1982).

implication is evidently that there is a wider church beyond England. Furthermore, unlike most of the continental churches, the Church of England also kept – probably rather accidentally[22] – its own version of the threefold ministry of the pre-Reformation Church. This understanding of the catholic dimension of the Church of England has been retained to the present day. The preface to the declaration of assent, for example, which is said by all those taking up an ecclesiastical office, declares the Church of England to be 'part of the One, Holy, Catholic and Apostolic Church worshipping the one true God, Father, Son and Holy Spirit'. However, precisely how this catholicity is to be expressed remains unclear: even today, according to the terms of the English establishment, the final authority over the Church is still the English sovereign, although most of the 'imperial' powers have been delegated to parliament and more recently to the General Synod. Nevertheless, the scope of extra-provincial authority is severely curtailed by the effects of establishment and the theory of a national independent Church. What this represents is a very different model of catholicity from represented by the Roman Catholic Church. This can be well illustrated from the debates with Roman Catholics that took place in the reign of Elizabeth I.

Apologetics and the Papacy

In the early period of Anglican apologetics, particularly with the formulations following the Elizabethan Settlement of religion after the reign of Mary I, this problem of how a national Church could also be catholic became one of the most

---

22 See Mark D. Chapman, 'The Politics of Episcopacy' in *Bishops, Saints and Politics* (London: T&T Clark, 2007), pp. 9–32; German translation: 'Bischofsamt und Politik' in *Zeitschrift für Theologie und Kirche* 97:4 (2000), pp. 434–62. Also in Ingolf U. Dalferth (ed.), *Einheit bezeugen/Witnessing to Unity*, Frankfurt am Main, 2004, pp. 170–97.

important aspects of the self-definition of the Church of England. What was key was that catholicity could never be conferred by being in communion with the universal primate, nor indeed with any other bishop outside England, but had to be located somewhere else. The foremost figure in this process of self-definition was John Jewel (1522–71), Bishop of Salisbury from 1560. As bishop-elect he preached a sermon where he challenged his Roman Catholic opponents 'to bring any one sufficient sentence out of old Catholicke Doctor, or Father; or out of any old Generell Councell; Or out of the Holy Scriptures of God' to justify their practices.[23] Jewel's claim was that the Church of England was the true inheritor of the apostolic and early Church and had returned to the purity of the past. He developed this theme in his *Apologia Ecclesiae Anglicanae*, which became the semi-official theology of the Church of England in the reign of James I.

Jewel justified the abolition of certain abuses in the Church by citing the Fathers and scripture. He thus sought to 'shew it plain, that God's holy Gospel, the ancient bishops, and the primitive Church do make on our side, and that we have not without just cause left these men, and rather have returned to the apostles and old catholic fathers'.[24] The counterbalance was consequently to show that the Church of Rome had 'forsaken the fellowship of the Holy Fathers'.[25] Arguing against Roman Primacy, Jewel directly challenged the Pope:

---

23 *The Works of Bishop John Jewel* (Cambridge: Cambridge University Press for the Parker Society (PS), 1845–50), 4 vols, I, p. 20. On the use of the Fathers in Anglican theology, see Jean-Louis Quantain, *The Church of England and Christian Antiquity: The Construction of a Confessional Identity in the 17th Century* (Oxford: Oxford University Press, 2009).

24 PS III, p. 56.

25 PS IV, p. 901.

> Tell us, I pray you, good holy Father, seeing ye do crake so
> much of all antiquity, and boast yourself that all men are bound
> to you alone, which of all the fathers have at any time called
> you by the name of the highest prelate, the universal bishop, or
> the head of the Church? Which of them ever said that both the
> swords were committed to you?[26]

Jewel addresses this question by turning to the writings of the
Fathers to defend his own Church:

> As for our doctrine, which we might rightlier call Christ's
> catholic doctrine, it is so far off from new, that God, who is
> above all most ancient, and the Father of our Lord Jesus Christ.
> ... So that no man can now think our doctrine to be new, unless
> the same think either the prophets' faith, or the Gospel, or else
> Christ himself to be new.[27]

Here Jewel develops an understanding of what can be called
the 'temporal' catholicity implicit in the English Reformation.
Catholicity is understood through a return to the past rather
than as something conferred by any visible institution in the
present.

In the years that followed a similar method came to be
adopted by figures from across the theological spectrum. In the
next century, for instance, William Laud, Archbishop of Canterbury executed in 1644, developed a theology of the limited
nature of provincial authority,[28] a theme that had been
enunciated in the Thirty-nine Articles (Art. 21), which stated
that all institutions of the Church can err. Laud claimed that 'if
a General Council will go out of the Church's way, it may

---

26 PS I, p. 43.

27 PS I, p. 39.

28 'A Relation of the Conference between William Laud and Mr Fisher
    the Jesuit', in *The Works of William Laud* (Oxford: Parker, 1849), ii,
    p. 247.

easily go without the Church's truth'.[29] He was keen to emphasize that since no one part of the church was free from error, each church was free to make its own decisions as long as it was in obedience to the rule of scripture.[30] Laud thereby develops a theory of the autonomy of the local church, which had a duty to reform itself:[31]

> [W]hen the universal church will not, or for the iniquities of the times cannot, obtain and settle a free General Council, it is lawful, nay sometimes necessary, to reform gross abuses by a national, or a provincial.[32]

Since there can be no universal teaching office exempt from error, Laud claims, provincial councils have the duty to 'decree in causes of faith, and in cases of reformation, where corruptions have crept into the sacraments of Christ'.[33] Laud develops this idea further by limiting the claims of all other bishops. He thus suggests that the authority of the 'patriarch' of Rome is essentially the same as that of the other patriarchs, including the Archbishop of Canterbury, whose authority is equivalent to that of a patriarch.[34] There can be no appeal beyond the patriarch who is 'supreme in his own patriarchate'.[35] While the Bishop of Rome might have authority in Rome, it was impossible for his jurisdiction to be exercised over the whole Church, since this would threaten the claims of the local church (as well as the king's sovereignty).[36] This understanding of provincial autonomy was often defended

---

29 'Conference', p. 266.
30 'Conference', p.366.
31 'Conference', p. 235.
32 'Conference', p. 170.
33 'Conference', p. 171.
34 'Conference', p. 190.
35 'Conference', p. 189.
36 'Conference', p. 225.

using the example of St Cyprian:[37] indeed, it comes as little surprise that Peter Heylyn gave his hagiographical biography of Laud the title *Cyprianus Anglicus*.[38] This means that each church expresses a form of 'contained catholicity' in only very loose connection with other churches.[39]

Tradition and Development

There were obvious implications in this theology of 'temporal catholicity' which was related to a national Church for the understanding of tradition: where there could be no authoritative living voice then tradition was understood as something fixed and finalized in the teaching of the Church of the first four or so centuries, which was always related to scripture as the final arbiter in doctrinal dispute.[40] Authority could not be located in the present, either in Pope or Council. In one of his important Anglican writings, Newman clearly enunciated the difference between a Roman Catholic and an

---

37 See 'Cyprianus Anglicus: St Cyprian in Anglican Interpretation' in *Bishops, Saints and Politics*, pp. 33–52. On this, see my essay, 'Catholicity, Unity and Provincial Autonomy: On Making Decisions Unilaterally', in *Anglican Theological Review* 76 (1994), pp. 313–28.

38 Peter Heylyn, *Cyprianus Anglicus or, The History of the Life and Death of the Most Revered and Renowned Prelate William, by Divine Providence, Lord Archbishop of Canterbury* (London: A. Seile, 1668).

39 See esp. 'From Carthage to Truro: Archbishop Benson and the Unity of the Church' in *Bishops, Saints and Politics*, pp. 53–65.

40 The classic recent formulation of this theology is by Michael Ramsey, *The Gospel and the Catholic Church* (London: Longmans, Green and Co., 1937), p. 180. The Catholic Church is constantly under judgement; its subjects its pride to the humiliation of the cross. 'these are Catholicism's own themes, and out of them it was born. But they are themes learnt and relearnt in humiliation, and Catholicism always stands before the Church door at Wittenberg to read the truth by which she is created and by which she is to be judged' (p. 180).

Anglican understanding of tradition. Adopting a method similar to his intellectual forebears, he suggested that even though the Church of Rome may

> profess a reverence for Antiquity, she does not really feel and pay it. There are, in fact, two elements in operation within her system. As far as it is Catholic and Scriptural, it appeals to the Fathers; as far as it is a corruption, it finds it necessary to supersede them. Viewed in its formal principles and authoritative statements, it professes to be the champion of past times; viewed as an active and political power, as a ruling, grasping, ambitious principle, in a word, as what is expressively called popery, it exalts the will and pleasure of the existing Church above all authority, whether of Scripture or Antiquity, interpreting the one and disposing of the other by its absolute and arbitrary decree.[41]

According to the Newman of the early days of the Oxford Movement, Roman Catholicism exalts the present at the expense of the past revelation found in scripture, which had functioned as the sole doctrinal norm for the Church of England.[42] Newman, like the other leaders of the Catholic revival in the Church of England, sought to purify their church by returning to the past. In his sermon on *Primitive Tradition*, for instance, Keble limited tradition solely to

> those rules, in which *all* primitive Councils are uniform, those rites and formularies which are found in *all* primitive liturgies, and those interpretations and principles of interpretation in which *all* orthodox Fathers agree … genuine canons of the primitive Councils, and the genuine fragments of the primitive

---

41 J. H. Newman, *Lectures on the Prophetical Office of the Church* (Oxford: Parker 1837), p. 100.

42 See Peter Nockles, *The Oxford Movement in Context: Anglican High Churchmanship, 1760–1857* (Cambridge: Cambridge University Press, 1993), ch. 2.

> Liturgies, are reducible into a small space; even although we go
> so low down in both as the division of the Eastern and Western
> Churches, including the six first Councils general, and
> excluding image-worship and similar corruptions by authority.[43]

Such a temporal conception of catholicity differentiated the
Church of England from the Roman Catholic Church, with its
very different understanding of tradition.

In a more recent piece of polemic, the Irish Bishop Richard
Hanson noted that the Roman Catholic 'religion is a religion
which looks to the present, and to the future for its revelation,
indeed one which may confidently expect new revelations and
new fundamental doctrines of Christianity to emerge in the
future into public gaze'. Because of this, according to Hanson,
it had 'reversed the current of original faith'. For Anglicans,
development was quite different from innovation, and could
take place 'only in the enunciation of certain formulae
necessary to protect the original tradition of the Church from
error'.[44] For such thinkers, without an authoritative teaching
office there could be no development of doctrine, even though
the original deposit would have to be expressed afresh in every
generation.[45] Instead, all development was to be subjected to

---

43 John Keble, *Primitive Tradition Recognised in Holy Scripture* (London:
Rivington, 1836), p. 40.

44 R. P. C. Hanson and R. Fuller, *The Church of Rome. A Dissuasive*
(London: SCM Press, 1948), pp. 84, 102.

45 See also, R. P. C. Hanson, *Tradition in the Early Church* (London:
SCM Press, 1963). On development see the classic discussion by
Owen Chadwick, *From Bossuet to Newman* (Cambridge: Cambridge
University Press, second edition 1987); and Aidan Nichols OP, *From
Newman to Congar: The Idea of Doctrinal Development from the Victorians
to the Second Vatican Council* (Edinburgh: T&T Clark, 1990), pp. 1-16.

criticism, and could never be final and absolute. The Anglican response was thus one of humility and openness.[46]

ARCIC, Catholicity, and Primacy

These historical illustrations, which are obviously far from comprehensive, reveal something of the complexity of the problems arising from the issue of catholicity in Anglican theology. It is also clear that Roman Catholic and Anglican conceptions of the nature of catholicity and of tradition and development are profoundly different. However, while this difference was acknowledged in the two ARCIC reports on authority, as well as in the report, *The Gift of Authority: Authority in the Church III* from ARCIC II,[47] it was not seen to be insurmountable. Thus in the first report on Authority, the individual bishop's office was understood as that of connecting the local church with the 'universal communion of which it is part'.[48] The Petrine office is regarded as an extension of this office which co-ordinates all churches: 'Communion with him is intended as a safeguard of the catholicity of all the churches.'[49]

---

46 On this see the essays in Kenneth Stevenson (ed.), *A Fallible Church: Lambeth Essays* (London: Darton, Longman & Todd, 2008), esp. Mark D. Chapman, 'Where is it all going? A Plea for Humility', pp. 122–41.

47 *The Gift of Authority: Authority in the Church III* (An Agreed Statement by the Second Anglican–Roman Catholic International Commission) (London, Toronto and New York: CTS, Anglican Book Centre and Church Publishing, 1999). It is not clear to me that the work of ARCIC II has been able to act with the openness and trust that was demonstrated in ARCIC I which goes a long way to explaining why its reports have been largely ignored, at least in much of the Anglican Communion.

48 'Authority I', §8 (p. 45).

49 'Authority I', §12 (p. 47); cf. §23 (p. 52).

The problems over primacy and infallibility were discussed further in the second report, which noted the significant agreement over the need for some form of primacy:

> If the leadership of the bishop of Rome has been rejected by those who thought it was not faithful to the truth of the Gospel and hence not a true focus of unity, we nevertheless agree that a universal primacy will be needed in a reunited Church and should appropriately be the primacy of the bishop of Rome.[50]

The Petrine Office would function in a reunited Church as a 'sign and safeguard' of the 'visible koinonia' of the unity present in the company of faithful believers.[51] However, the report went on to claim:

> The doctrine that a universal primacy expresses the will of God does not entail the consequence that a Christian community out of communion with the see of Rome does not belong to the Church of God. Being in canonical communion with the bishop of Rome is not among the necessary elements by which a Christian community is recognized as a church.[52]

This could be perceived as a major concession from the Roman Catholic side: communion with the papacy was not an absolute requirement for a true Church. Similarly, it was acknowledged that the language of divine right used at Vatican One need no longer be regarded as a matter of disagreement.[53] In turn, the universal primate was to exercise his ministry only 'in collegial association with his brother bishops'.[54]

---

50 'Authority II', §9 (p. 65).
51 'Authority II', §11 (p. 66).
52 'Authority II', §12 (p. 66).
53 'Authority II', §13 (p. 67).
54 'Authority II', §21 (p. 69); cf. 'Authority I' §§21, 23 (pp. 51, 52).

With regard to infallibility, there was a recognition that the Church 'can in a matter of essential doctrine make a decisive judgement which becomes part of its permanent witness', but at the same time, the report noted that:

> The purpose of this service cannot be to add to the content of revelation, but is to recall and emphasize some important truth; to expound the faith more lucidly; to expose error; to draw out implications not sufficiently recognized; and to show how Christian truth applies to contemporary issues.[55]

Most importantly, perhaps, the report claimed that

> The Church's teaching authority is a service to which the faithful look for guidance especially in times of uncertainty; but the assurance of the truthfulness of its teaching rests ultimately rather upon its fidelity to the Gospel than upon the character or office of the person by whom it is expressed. The Church's teaching is proclaimed because it is true; it is not true simply because it has been proclaimed. The value of such authoritative proclamation lies in the guidance that it gives to the faithful. However, neither general councils nor universal primates are invariably preserved from error even in official declarations.[56]

In what could appear as a threat to the doctrine of infallibility the report asserted: 'If the definition proposed for assent were not manifestly a legitimate interpretation of biblical faith and in line with orthodox tradition, Anglicans would think it a duty to reserve the reception of the definition for study and discussion.'[57] What becomes clear in reading the two reports on authority, together with the vigorous responses from the Roman Catholic side, is the contentious nature of the Petrine

---

55   'Authority II', §27 (p. 71).

56   'Authority II', §27 (p. 72).

57   'Authority II', §29 (p. 73).

office within the Roman Catholic Church itself: the Church of England's ambivalence towards universal primacy has highlighted issues faced by the Roman Catholic Church over the relationship between collegiality and universal primacy. A move towards a more limited understanding of the Church threatened the hermeneutics of unity. Indeed, for many Roman Catholics ecumenism is addressed as much internally as externally.[58] Not surprisingly, many Roman Catholic critics, including Cardinal Joseph Ratzinger, were deeply wary of the ARCIC Final Report because of these apparent concessions to a very different model of catholicity.

It is also important to note that the ARCIC process revealed the extraordinarily limited and undeveloped concept of a teaching office in the Anglican Communion. If the logic of the Anglican position is that tradition has to be fixed in the past, with the implication that doctrinal development is complete, then there can be no authority capable of definitive decision-making powers short of an ecumenical council. The problem that emerges, however, is over precisely what sort of authority is capable of making decisions in the present, especially when conflict arises. Within the confines of a national Church, this does not necessarily present insurmountable problems – there

---

58 There are strong resonances here of the debates between Ratzinger and Cardinal Walter Kasper over the relationship between universal and particular churches. The Ratzinger/Kasper debate: the universal church and local churches. The debate was set off by the letter issued by the Congregation for the Doctrine of the Faith, *Letter to the Bishops of the Catholic Church on Some Aspects of the Church understood as Communion* (25 June 1992) at: http://www.vatican.va/roman_curia/congregations/cfaith/documents/rc_con_cfaith_doc_2805199 2_communionis-notio_en.html (accessed 28 August 2009). For a synopsis and review of the debate, see Kilian McDonnell OSB, 'The Ratzinger/Kasper Debate: The Universal Church and Local Churches', *Theological Studies* 63 (2002), pp. 227–50.

can be clearly demarcated systems of decision-making. The issues between the churches, however, are very different. Recent debates within the Anglican Communion, especially those in the summer of 2008,[59] can perhaps best be understood as an attempt to develop a form of catholicity out of the loose authority structures of Anglicanism. Given the traditional Anglican approach to tradition and authority, this is likely to be quite different from the form of infallibility represented by the Roman Catholic model which centralizes the authority of the Church in a universal teaching office. While the Roman Catholic model would be completely unacceptable to all but a handful of eccentric Anglo-Catholics of the anglo-Papalist variety,[60] the recent divisions in the Communion reveal the tensions that can arise from the absence of a definitive teaching office at least on a global level, and the need for some sort of inter-provincial system of authority in conflict resolution.

GAFCON and Catholicity

While obviously the presenting issue in the recent debates in the Anglican Communion has been over the compatibility of homosexual practice with ordination and the related issue of the use of scripture, the ecclesiological question of the relationship between the national Church and the international communion remains fundamental. Unconstrained unilateral action is a particularly prized possession of some of the Anglican provinces. However, by its very nature as something transnational, catholicity refuses to be contained in practice within the confines of the provincial or national churches. For

---

59 I have discussed this at length in my introduction to Mark Chapman, Martyn Percy, Barney Hawkins and Ian Markham (eds), *Christ and Culture: Communion After Lambeth (Canterbury Studies in Anglicanism)* (Norwich: Canterbury Press, 2010).

60 On this, see Michael Yelton, *Anglican Papalism* (Norwich: Canterbury Press, 2005).

some Anglicans it is clear that the best way forward is to define Anglicanism more rigidly and prescriptively, and to ensure that churches subscribe to a set of doctrinal propositions as the mark of what counts as authentic catholicity. Many of the approximately 289 bishops (or 'pilgrims' as they called themselves) who met in Jerusalem at the Global Anglican Future Conference (GAFCON) shortly before the Lambeth Conference were evidently dissatisfied with the slow progress being made in the development of some sort of mechanism for conflict resolution and mutual acknowledgement of extra-provincial authority. On their view, the moves towards an Anglican Covenant were far too tentative and lacked a clear doctrinal authority.[61] Without wishing to rehearse the strongly dualist language of spiritual warfare which was used by the primate of Nigeria, Peter Akinola, at the GAFCON Conference, I think it is nevertheless important to note the conception of catholicity at work in Jerusalem. The lack of a teaching office proved disastrous for the authenticity of the Christian Faith.[62] The instruments of unity did little more than promote disunity: the strong words of the resolutions made by the Lambeth Conference and the primates after 1998 had been ignored and trivialized by the official structures of the Anglican Communion. What the GAFCON bishops called for was a new structure to control membership through a far tighter definition of catholicity. For them, catholicity was not restricted to national boundaries nor the past, but is modelled on doctrinal purity upheld by a confession of faith. Ironically, perhaps, given their emphasis on Reformation principles, their

---

61 On the covenant, see Mark D. Chapman (ed.), *The Anglican Covenant: Unity and Diversity in the Anglican Communion* (London: Mowbray, 2008).

62 Peter Akinola, opening address at GAFCON, 22 June 2008 at: http://www.gafcon.org/index.php?option=com_content&task=view&id=57&Itemid=29

goal is far closer to the tightly controlled curial model of modern Roman Catholicism.

Conclusion

There are a number of important points that emerge from this discussion of catholicity. First, and perhaps most important, is an awareness of the profoundly different ways in which catholicity can be understood. As the debates between Anglicans and Roman Catholics through history and in the ARCIC process demonstrate, catholicity carries with it implications for the understanding of tradition and authority. On the one hand, for Anglicanism, the odd combination of politics and theology that characterized the English Reformation meant that a visible teaching office scarcely existed. For Roman Catholicism, on the other hand, the Church has been defined in terms of communion with the holder of the universal teaching office. This fundamental difference, which was clearly emphasized by the present Pope (in his former guise) with his stress on the 'hermeneutics of unity',[63] makes ecumenism extremely precarious.[64]

Secondly, the history of Anglican theology reveals the origins of the problems facing the Communion in coming to terms with its sense of being a worldwide catholic church. The globalization of the idea of national churches has led to an

---

63 'Anglican–Catholic Dialogue – Its Problems and Hopes (1983)', in Christopher Hill and Edward Yarnold SJ (eds), *Anglicans and Roman Catholics: The Search for Unity* (London: SPCK/CTS, 1994), pp. 251–82, here p. 267. See also *Dominus Iesus* (October 2000), §16 at: http://www.vatican.va/roman_curia/congregations/cfaith/docume nts/rc_con_cfaith_doc_20000806_dominus-iesus_en.html.

64 On the future of Anglican ecumenism, see the collection edited by Paul Avis, *Paths to Unity: Explorations in Ecumenical Method* (London: Church House Publishing, 2004).

extraordinarily weak system of inter-provincial authority in the Anglican Communion.[65] The so-called instruments of unity – the Lambeth Conference, the Anglican Consultative Council, the Primates' Meeting and the Archbishop of Canterbury himself – have virtually no intrinsic authority. This means that there is no real mechanism for conflict resolution, which is why the Anglican Covenant – as a starting point for a spatial concept of catholicity – has become so crucial for the survival of the worldwide communion.[66] But recent events in the American Episcopal Church, which has recently lifted a moratorium on the election of gay bishops,[67] as well as the Archbishop of Canterbury's response,[68] indicate clearly the problem of 'contained' and purely temporal versions of catholicity. Anglicans are all too aware that pluralism carries with it the danger of anarchy and schism. But most wish to resist centralized views of catholicity. For this reason it is not clear to me precisely how worldwide Anglicanism will develop into *one* catholic Church.

65 For a brief account see my *Anglicanism: A Very Short Introduction* (Oxford: Oxford University Press, 2006), chs 6 and 7.

66 See the essays in Mark D. Chapman (ed.), *The Anglican Covenant*, esp. ch. 1.

67 See the press release at the end of the General Convention at: http://www.episcopalchurch.org/79901_112765_ENG_HTM.htm (accessed 25 August 2009).

68 'Communion, Covenant and our Anglican Future' (27 July 2009) at: http://www.archbishopofcanterbury.org/2502 (accessed 25 August 2009).

7

Know Surrender: From Ulster to Windsor

MARTYN PERCY

One day, so the joke goes, the Archbishop of Canterbury is sitting alone on the beach, trying to enjoy a holiday and a retreat. It has been another hard year. He gazes out towards the horizon where the sun is still rising, and sighs. Presently, his eye catches something gleaming in the sand. He brushes away the grains, and pulls out a brass canister. Seeing an inscription, he spits on it and polishes it, but before he can read it, the canister explodes in a haze of blue smoke. The Archbishop rubs his eyes, and is surprised to find, standing before him, a large Genie. 'Your Grace', says the Genie, 'I will grant you one wish – whatever you want: just name it.' The Archbishop reaches inside his cassock pocket, and pulls out a map of the Middle East. With a crayon, he draws a large red circle around the whole area. 'I'd like you to bring peace to this region', he says. The Genie does not reply. He sits on the sand, and looks at the rising sun. He says nothing for ten minutes. Then, turning again to the Archbishop, he says: 'I have never said this to anyone before, but what you ask is beyond me. It is too difficult. But if you have another wish, I will grant that.' The Archbishop pauses, and then reaches inside for another map. This is a map of the world, with 165 countries coloured in. 'This is the Anglican Communion', says the Archbishop, 'and all I ask is that you help all the many different parts to get on a little better.' The Genie sits back down on the sand again, and looks towards the sun. Again, for ten minutes, he says nothing. Then he stands up, and turns to the Archbishop. 'Your Grace', he says, 'do you think I could have another look at that first map?'

Just for a moment, close your eyes. Not literally, obviously; the rest of the essay could not be read if you did so. I mean metaphorically. And, for a moment, imagine a world – an ecclesial world, if you will – in which Peter Akinola embraces Gene Robinson warmly. The two smile as they do so: the greeting is warm, tender and reciprocal. Looking on is the Archbishop of Sydney and the Presiding bishop of the American Episcopal Church (TEC). Their eyes also meet, smiling. Other bishops witnessing this break into warm, gentle applause. There is peace, harmony and happiness.

You may now be rubbing your eyes, rather in disbelief. Yes, it was a dream. And I suppose, not the kind that will be to everyone's liking. But, as you know, our Anglican polity is laced with frustrations and tensions:

> The Church of England is the maddening institution it is because that is how the English like their religion – pragmatic, comfortable and unobtrusive. Small wonder that so many English writers have preferred the dramatic certainties of Catholicism. You simply couldn't write a novel like Graham Greene's *The Power and the Glory* about a Church built on the conviction that anything can be settled over a cup of tea ... There are other Churches in Christendom which take pride in their lack of ambiguity – in doctrine ... or in monolithic interpretation of the Gospel. Anglicanism in contrast is a synthesis, and a synthesis necessarily invites thesis and antithesis.[1]

How does the proverb go? 'The first casualty in war is truth.' So, Anglicans, ought to be doubly concerned when wars, rumours of wars, along with legitimized schisms and rifts start

---

1   J. Paxman, *The English: Portrait of a People* (London: Penguin, 1999), p. 98.

to surface within the mother church of the Anglican Communion – the Church of England. Standing as we are now, in the twenty-first century, it is still not difficult to forget some of the ugly scenes that took place at the Lambeth Conference at Canterbury during the summer of 1998. In contrast, 2008 was a rather peaceable affair, though not without its pain, emphasized largely by boycotts and noises off stage rather than anything that might take centre stage.

But back to 1988 for a moment. On matters of sexuality in particular, the talk was of irrational fears, of a new strident conservatism, of an old and dominant liberalism, of traditionalism, homophobia or homosexuality, and of a split between North and South – reminiscent of the first Great Schism of over a thousand years ago, between the East and West. It seems to be the usual story. In spite of the many good and excellent things that were going on at Lambeth, the public were nevertheless presented with a picture of a communion that was unravelling, unable to keep itself together any more, agree on common services, ordination, consecration, and its own future. Things are falling apart: the centre cannot hold.

At that Conference, it was Rowan Williams, the then Bishop of Monmouth, who won the dubious award – gifted by Andrew Brown, a Religious Affairs Correspondent who writes for a number of newspapers – of having 'the most interesting failure' of the Conference. Williams gave a keynote address on making moral decisions. It was a lecture of considerable subtlety and some substance, which, for all the effect it had, Brown noted that 'he might as well have delivered it in a motorway service station'. After the lecture, Brown states that Williams commented: 'Wittgenstein said that the most important thing a philosopher can say to another is "give yourself time". The question is whether we can, in some sense, bear to keep talking to each other.'

From Ulster to Windsor

One of the chief virtues of living within a Communion is learning to be patient. Churches, each with their distinctive own intra-denominational familial identity, have to learn how to negotiate the differences they find within themselves. For some churches in recent history, the discovery of such differences – perhaps on matters of authority, praxis or interpretation – has been too much to bear: lines have been drawn in the sand, with the sand itself serving only as a metaphor for the subsequent atomization. Yet typically, most mainstream Protestant denominations have sufficient breadth (of viewpoints and plurality) and depth (located in sources of authority and their interpretation, amongst other things) to be able to resist those assaults that threaten implosion. Where some new churches, faced with internal disagreement, have quickly experienced fragmentation, most historic denominations have been reflexive enough to experience little more than a process of elastication: they have been stretched, but they have not broken. This is perhaps inevitable, when one considers the global nature of most mainstream historic denominations. Their very expanse will have involved a process of stretching (missiological, moral, conversational, hermeneutical, etc.), and this in turn has led directly to their (often inchoate) sense of accommodation.

This is, of course, not to say that 'anything goes'. Even the broadest and most accommodating ecclesial traditions have their boundaries and limits. But the development of their global identity has involved them in a process of patient listening and learning, and of evolution and devolution. Speaking as an Anglican, therefore (and one who would locate himself in the broad 'centre' of the tradition), I hesitate to begin this brief essay by confessing that I am continually surprised by the amount of passion and rhetoric that has been created by the issue of homosexuality. In three successive movements (in what must pass for, musicologically, as both a tragic and comic opera), the Anglican Communion has threatened to unravel itself over arrangements in Canada, the USA and England. The historical minutiae of those events in the dioceses of New Westminster, New Hampshire and Oxford have no need of reprise now, for they have each, in their own way, been responsible for the production of yet another Commission that attempts to deal with the (apparently) self-inflicted wounds that are said to afflict the Communion. And now that the *Windsor Report* has been published, it is interesting to note that one of its primary tasks has been to point towards the importance of listening to one another in that school of theology, which is the learning Church.

Broadly speaking, I consider the *Windsor Report* to be a fine piece of Anglican apologetics. Under the skilful chairing of Robert Eames, Archbishop of Armagh – a man who through his own painful experiences of the 'Ulster Problem' knows a thing or two about patience, peace processes and reconciliation – the report manages to keep open the possibility of a future in which those people who profoundly disagree on some issues can nonetheless continue to regard themselves as being together and in Communion, even if the quality of that belonging is more strained than usual. In the process of its deliberations, the Commission, by any standards, set itself an ambitious question: what do we believe is the will of God for the Anglican Communion? In attempting to address the central issue, the members of the Commission have been well aware that:

> Since the 1970s controversies over issues of human sexuality have become increasingly divisive and destructive throughout Christendom. Within the Anglican Communion the intensity of debate on these issues at successive Lambeth Conferences has

demonstrated the reality of these divisions ... Voices and declarations have portrayed a Communion in crisis. Those divisions have been obvious at several levels of Anglican life: between provinces, between dioceses and between individual Anglican clergy and laity. The popular identification of 'conservatives' and 'liberals', and 'the west' as opposed to 'the global south', has become an over-simplification – divisions of opinion have also become clear within provinces, dioceses and parishes. Various statements and decisions at different levels of leadership and membership of the Church have illustrated the depth of reaction. Among other Christian traditions, reactions to the problems within Anglicanism have underlined the serious concerns on these issues worldwide. Comparison has been made with the controversies on women's ordination years ago. But the current strengths of expression of divergent positions are much greater. Questions have been raised about the nature of authority in the Anglican Communion, the inter-relationship of the traditional Instruments of Unity, the ways in which Holy Scripture is interpreted by Anglicans, the priorities of the historic autonomy enshrined in Anglican provinces, and there are also issues of justice. Yet the Lambeth Commission has been aware that consideration within its mandate of any specific aspect of inter-Anglican relationships overlaps and relates to others and has a clear bearing on the sort of Anglican Communion which should enhance the life and worship of our diverse worldwide church family.[2]

Perhaps unusually for a Commission that deals with contested areas within ecclesiology, The *Windsor Report* gives particular prominence to the 'feelings', 'emotions' and 'passions' that the issue of sexuality raises. Even in the Foreword, words and phrases such as 'intensity', 'depth of feeling' and 'depth of conviction' pepper the pages. Eames notes that the 'harshness' and 'lack of charity' that has sometimes characterized the debate is 'new to Anglicanism'.

---

2   *The Windsor Report* (London: Anglican Communion Office, 2004), foreword.

Perhaps for this reason alone (although there are others), Eames is careful to note that:

> This Report is not a judgement. It is part of a process. It is part of a pilgrimage towards healing and reconciliation. The proposals which follow attempt to look forward rather than merely to recount how difficulties have arisen.

The process proposed by the *Windsor Report*, is of course, one predicated on a shared commitment to patience, listening and learning together. In order to maintain the bonds of affection that are vital to the life of the Communion, it will be necessary for each part of the body to act with restraint and courtesy. Thus, the report affirms 'the importance of interdependence', whilst also acknowledging that Communion has been breached through particular initiatives, which are specifically identified and spoken of in terms of 'regret'. The Commission proposes to resolve the ensuing disputes through a period of calm and continued dialogue, with all parties urged 'to seek ways of reconciliation'. The *Windsor Report* concludes on an upbeat-yet-sanguine note, calling for peace, patience, restraint and healing, earnestly setting forth a continued faith in a Communion, in which the participants choose to walk together for the sake of unity, and for its witness to the gospel.

Can We Talk?

So to return to Wittgenstein's question, 'can we still talk to each other?' The earlier mention of Eames and Ulster is not accidental. Northern Ireland has seen some of the most bitter civil strife and violence over the last century, and much of it predicated on religious difference. Yet somehow, the province has come together, and the violence abated, and the possibility of deep and lasting peace established. The 'Balkanization' of the province – dividing the places and peoples into smaller autonomous self-governing entities – has been avoided. There are many, of course, who would seek exactly that future with the Anglican Communion: third provinces, exclusions, and so forth. In effect, an attempt to create an array of small 'safe' ecclesial homelands that no longer relate to neighbours. But the Communion, of course, is fiercely resistant to such Balkanisation. It knows in its soul that the sum is greater than the part; that the catholic whole is to be preferred to an assemblage of parts that are each sure of their own individual righteousness. Northern Ireland has taught us that peace with our neighbour (so yes, our enemy) is worth struggling for, and that independence from each other is a lesser vision.

So how might a fusion of political, emotional and ecclesial intelligence offer some kind of indicative pathway ahead for the Anglican Communion? Several things can be said. And in order to earth these brief ecclesial reflections more substantially, I am drawing upon the first-hand account of the peace-making process in Northern Ireland, written by Jonathan Powell. In *Great Hatred, Little Room*,[3] Powell hints at several instructive, mediating, yet temporary paradigms that have implications for theology and ecclesiology. Here again, and for illustrative purposes our attention is drawn to current difficulties in Anglican polity.

First, Powell notes how the uses of 'constructive ambiguity' can help establish conversation and rapport at the early stages of negotiation. In one sense, critics might say that this can mean two sides talking two slightly different languages. Speaking is taking place, but true listening is more limited than it may appear to be. Powell concedes that constructive ambig-

---

3   Jonathan Powell, *Great Hatred, Little Room: Making Peace in Northern Ireland* (London: Bodley Head, 2008). The title of the book is taken from W. B. Yeats's poem, 'Remorse for Intemperate Speech', 1931.

uity is fine for the beginning of a peace process, but not enough in the middle and end stages. Ambiguity has to be rejected in favour of clarity.

Second, Powell notes how consensus must be built from the centre. Again, this is vital to begin with. But you have to reconcile opposites. So for Anglicans, the Archbishop of Canterbury – or other instruments of unity – may be able to hold together competing convictions for some while. In effect, 'manage diversity'. But in the end, there is no substitute for the ultimacy of Peter Akinola shaking hands with Gene Robinson; or for Peter Jensen sitting down with Katherine Jefferts Schori. Whilst this may be hard to imagine, it is the kind of 'peace' that is anticipated in God's Kingdom; the end of rhetorical violence, and the ushering in of a community of blessing and consensus that transcends mere consensus.

Third, Powell's insights suggest that the fragmentation and 'Balkanization' of polity is to be avoided at all costs, because it is difficult if not impossible to build consensus out of brokenness. In ecclesiological terms, if you have the choice between heresy and schism, choose heresy. You can correct the former; but it will always be difficult to ever heal the latter. This lays a particular burden on the identity and role for the so-called 'instruments of unity': the Archbishop of Canterbury, the Primates, the Anglican Consultative Council and the Lambeth Conference. The instruments will need to act lightly and precisely, lest they become part of the problem.

Fourth, these instruments of unity and peace may need to triangulate in times of crisis: it is not good hovering between passive-aggressive; liberal-conservative; traditional-progressive modes of behaviours. It will be necessary to get beyond these polarities; and for the instruments to become *facilitators of peace*, not mere persuaders for a temporary cessation in hostilities. The difference is crucial, clearly. But as Powell notes, bringing peace takes time, and necessarily involves setbacks.

Underpinning this must be a resolute commitment to talking and listening – without which peace is impossible. And as the Church is a community of peace, attentive listening to God, self and otherness is at the core of its very being.

Fifth, the exchange of peace is a central act of preparation and declaration in anticipation of receiving Christ in bread and wine. Communion is centred on companionship – literally, 'those we break bread with'. Because of this, compromise – literally to 'promise together' – is something rooted in the heart of the Eucharist as we pledge ourselves to one another and to God. In accepting the consequential company that our ecclesial belief and behaviour brings us, we commit to a form of unity that is predicated on peace and bound for unity. That form of Communion, of course, does not always mean agreement. Nor does it follow that there will never be anger and division. But because of God's economy of blessing, it remains the case that no 'height or depth' (cf., Romans 8) can separate us from the love of God that is found in Jesus Christ. And because of this – God's ultimate purpose for creation – we cannot be separated from one another.

But the last word in this section belongs to Powell, as he reflects on the long and arduous road to peace in Northern Ireland. His reflections are instructive for all those who seek peace and unity in any context, including those wracked by the pain of ecclesial conflict, where there can often seem to be no hope of peaceful resolution, let alone unity:

> The ambiguity that had been essential at the beginning [of the process] began to undermine the Agreement and discredit the government – the referee for its implementation. We then had to drive ambiguity out of the process ... and insist on deeds rather than words. This process of squeezing out the ambiguity and building trust was painful and it took time, but a durable peace cannot rest on an ambiguous understanding ...

So if there is one lesson to be drawn from the Northern Ireland negotiations, it is that there is no reason to believe that efforts to find peace will fail just because they have failed before. You have to keep the wheels turning. The road to success in Northern Ireland was littered with failures. [But] there is every reason to think that the search for peace can succeed in other places where the process has encountered problems ... if people are prepared to talk.[4]

But, what kind of talk? According to Peter Kevern,[5] there is a reciprocal relationship between ecclesiology and practice in the Church of England. Logical arguments are invoked in support of a given course of action; conversely, pragmatic positions adopted by the Church eventually find expression as ecclesiological arguments. The debate on women's ordination represents an anomalous instance of this process, because it has resulted in two parallel 'integrities'. Each integrity has separate beliefs about the wisdom of such ordinations, backed up in both cases by a range of internally coherent ecclesiological positions. Those of the opponents of women's ordination are on the whole, less widely noted, and less lucidly expressed.

Partly due to the fragile nature of the communion at present, and also to a rather odd enclave mentality, the practical beliefs of the two integrities are mutually exclusive. Of course, these ecclesiologies have far more in common than is immediately apparent. As I have argued before, Anglicanism is carried in a kind of kinship – a sort of familial morphology in which mutual recognition is often quickly discerned.[6] There is initial

---

4   Powell, *Great Hatred*, pp. 315, 322.

5   Peter Kevern, 'Unity, Diversity and Trinity in the Rhetoric of the 1998 Lambeth Conference', PhD Thesis, University of Birmingham, 1999.

6   M. Percy, *Power and the Church: Ecclesiology in an Age of Transition* (London: Cassell, 1998), pp. 163ff.

evidence for this, in the fact that of those opposing the ordination of women, few have abandoned Church of England, despite losing the debate. Oddly, both sides profess to share a structured way of thinking about the Church, a meta-ecclesiology, in which both wings and the centre recognize something of the other, even if they are so far not giving formal expression to it. This all sounds very serious on one level, yet it perhaps pays to recall James Gordon Melton's sociological treatment of churches in terms of 'families'. For all the protestations of Forward in Faith, or proponents of Third Provinces, it is simply not very easy for your average Anglo-Catholic to feel 'at home' in Roman Catholicism.[7]

Passion, Polity and Power

As we noted earlier, it was Jeremy Paxman who once quipped that the Church of England is the kind of body that believes that there was no issue that could not be eventually solved over a cup of tea in the Vicar's study. This waspish compliment directed towards Anglican polity serves to remind us that many regard its ecclesial praxis as being quintessentially peaceable and polite, in which matters never really get to out of hand. For similar reasons, Robert Runcie once described Anglican polity as a matter of 'passionate coolness'. In the past, and in my own reflections on Anglican polity, these are sentiments with which I have tended to concur:

> In some of my conversations with Anglican theologians … I have been struck by how much of the coherence of Anglicanism depends on good manners. This sounds, at face value, like an extraordinarily elitist statement. It is clearly not meant to be that. What I mean by manners is learning to speak well, behave

---

7   J. Melton, *Encylopaedia of Religion in the USA* (Washington DC: Gale, 1978).

well, and be able to conduct yourself with integrity in the midst
of an argument ... It is often the case that in Anglicans' disputes
about doctrine, order or faith, it is actually the means that
matter more than the ends ... politeness, integrity, restraint,
diplomacy, patience, a willingness to listen, and above all, not
to be ill-mannered – these are the things that enable the
Anglican Communion to cohere.[8]

There can be no question that enabling ecclesial polity
depends, to some extent, on managing anger. In macro-
theological disputes, such as those over the ordination of
women, part of the strategy that enables unity can be centred
on muzzling some of the more passionate voices in the debate.
Extreme feelings, when voiced, can lead to extreme reactions.
And extreme reactions, when allowed full-vent, can make
situations unstable. Nations fall apart; Communions fracture;
families divide. Things said briefly in the heat of a moment can
cause wounds that may take years to heal. What is uttered is
not easily retracted.

Good manners, then, is not a bad analogy for 'ideal'
Anglican polity. In a Church that sets out to accommodate
many different peoples of every theological hue, there has to be
a foundation – no matter how implicit – that enables the
Communion to cohere across party lines, tribal borders and
doctrinal differences. And just as this is true for macro-
theological disputes, so is it also true for micro-ecclesial
squabbles. Keeping the peace in a congregation that is at
loggerheads over church fabric and fittings, or perhaps unable
to agree on an appropriate resolution in a complex ethical
debate, is a no less demanding task for a parish priest. Often,
congregational unity in the midst of disputes can only be
secured by finding a middle, open way, in which the voices of

---

8   M. Percy, 'On Sacrificing Purity?', in Ian Markham and Jan Jobling,
     Theological Liberalism (London, SPCK, 2000).

moderation and tolerance occupy the central ground and enable a Church to move forwards. In such situations, the cultivation of 'good manners' can be seen to be essential; civility quietly blossoms where arguments once threatened to lay waste. This is something that the *Windsor Report* understands, and it is interesting to note how much attention the report gives to the virtues of patience and restraint, whilst also acknowledging the place of passions and emotions in the sexuality debate. Clearly, there is a tension between these polarities (the polite-passionate axis), which is partly why the cultivation of 'mannered-ness' in ecclesial polity can be seen as being as essential as it is beguiling.

However, there are several important theological issues that surround this type of narration for a congregation, diocese, church or Communion, that tend to question its apparent wisdom. 'Good manners', for example, can be a form of quasi-pastoral *suppression* that does not allow true or strong feelings to emerge in the centre of an ecclesial community, and properly interrogate its 'settled' identity. This may rob the Church of the opportunity truly to feel the pain of those who may already perceive themselves to be on the margins of the Church, perhaps even disqualified, or who already feel silenced. 'Good manners' can also become a cipher for excluding the apparently undeserving, and perhaps labelling seemingly difficult insights as 'extreme voices'. The prophetic, the prescient, and those who protest, can all be ignored by a church that makes a virtue out of overly valuing a peaceable grammar of exchange. Put another way, if the 'coolness' always triumphs over the 'passionate', then the Church is effectively deaf in one ear.

Quite naturally therefore, there is the issue of anger itself, and of strong feelings – especially in relation to sexuality, on all sides of the debate – with which the *Windsor Report* is perhaps unusually concerned. In the Body of Christ, how are these feelings received, articulated and generated? Quite apart from appropriate 'righteous anger' (e.g., on matters of justice), how does a mature Church receive and respond to aggression within itself, and to strong feelings such as anger, dismay, passion, rage or enthusiasm? Rather like a good marital or parent–child relationship, learning to articulate and channel anger can be as important as learning to control it. It is often the case that in relationships where the expression of anger is denied its place, resentment festers and breeds, and true love is ultimately distorted. Strong feelings need to be acknowledged for relationships to flourish. If strong feelings on one or both sides have to be suppressed for the sake of a relationship, then it is rarely proper to speak of the relationship being mature or healthy. Indeed, some relationships that apparently present as being idyllic and peaceable (e.g., 'we never argue') can turn out to be pathologically problematic. Both parties, afraid of conflict and its consequences, deny their full truth to one another and themselves.

So in terms of ecclesial polity and pastoral praxis, the difficulty is this: the Church is too used to defining all aggression as negative. Correspondingly, the Church often fails to see the value of aggression or anger in the pursuit of just relations. Of course in retrospect we can acknowledge that freedoms for the oppressed have been won by aggressive behaviour, even when it has been militantly peaceful or pacifist: the Civil Rights movement in North America and the peaceful protests of Gandhi spring to mind. But all too often churches and society collude in a fiction, believing that an end to slavery, the emancipation of women, and perhaps even the end of apartheid, could all have been achieved without the aggressive behaviour of militants. Typically, the Church also fails to acknowledge the levels of inequality within itself. Many may still need to express or deploy aggressive behaviour in order for Kingdom values to be established.

139

Presently in the Church of England, the fear of conflict and aggression on issues of sexuality and gender makes it very difficult to air strong feelings; the neuralgic anxiety is that the manifestation of feelings leads to the loss of poise in ecclesial polity. And yet we live in a world and within a church that are shaped by human failings, and if we truly love these institutions then we will inevitably be angry about the ways they fall short. So what we Anglicans do with our strong feelings, and how we handle the aggression that moves for change, will depend on whether we can see them as a sign of life and growth, or whether we suppress them for fear they will rock the boat too hard.

In the Church, the desire to avoid conflict both in parochial matters and in relationships in the diocese can often be a recipe for atrophy. When situations arise which cannot be ignored, the scale of feelings aroused can surprise and disappoint those who believe that if we all try to love each other, we will all agree. To truly love is to take seriously the desire to deepen relationships and work against all that limits and devalues human worth. So discovering how to acknowledge and give voice to strong feelings – in ways that can enable radical working together for the growth of all – is a challenge that the Church needs to heed. In his ministry, Jesus consistently listened to the voices of the marginalized. Indeed, not only did he listen, but he assimilated such voices into his ministry, and often made the marginalized central, and placed those who were central on the periphery, thereby re-ordering society, forcing people to witness oppression and the response of the Kingdom of God to despair, anger and marginalization.

The task for the Church, therefore, is to find ways that do not to suppress or block out strong feelings of anger, or hurt and the aggression it arouses, but to help discern how to channel the energy they bring into the work of the gospel.[9] This means listening to the experiences that lead to aggression and anger, and seeing them as far as possible from the perspective of those with less power. It means humility on the part of those who hold power, and an acknowledgement of the fear of losing power and control. It means a new way of looking at power relationships that takes the gospel seriously in their equalizing and levelling.

The *Windsor Report*, therefore, is to be commended for the attention it pays to experiences and feelings. In recognizing their vital role in ecclesial polity, Eames and his colleagues on the Commission have understood that experiences and feelings need to be heard and received. The debate on sexuality (perhaps more so than that of gender?) is one that cannot be exclusively resolved by arid academic disputations. But this in itself raises a question about how the process of deliberation is to be furthered.

Coda

In an essay for the *Church Times* some years ago, Peter Selby noted that part of the cost of belonging to a church is 'sacrificing a straightforward confidence in our own purity'.[10] Communion is something that is necessarily shared, and correspondingly, we are all touched by one another's failures, and the necessary incompleteness of what constitutes church life. Selby's essay leans on the parable of the wheat and tares and presents a characteristically systematic and passionate plea

---

9 See for example Philip Groves, (ed), *The Anglican Communion and Homosexuality: A Resource to Enable Listening and Dialogue* (London: SPCK, 2008).

10 Peter Selby, 'The Parable of the Wheat and the Tares', *Church Times* (17 December 1999), p. 11.

for living together in tension, rather than trying to pre-empt the refining fire of God by building a pure Church on this side of the *parousia*. As he noted, situating the Church in that context, is not 'a plea for flaccid tolerance, let alone indifference on the matters of profound importance'. It is, on the other hand, a plea to try to try to work together as much as possible for the widest common good.

Our friends in Ulster would know a thing or two about this. That there is hope in hybridity, rather than risk and pollution. That in giving ourselves to one another – sacrificially, and in a spirit of surrender – we do not lose our fight, but rather find ourselves, and something higher, that Jesus calls us to in his Kingdom. That in knowing surrender, we do not taste defeat; but rather, begin to sense something of the victory of the resurrection, that triumphs over differences and disagreements, and begins to bring us all together in a new hope for the world. This is the Church, of course. A place and polity where we discover that in yielding to others, we do not lose our cause or the corner we have been fighting for. Rather, we gain more than we could have imagined. We find that in surrender, we are not defeated, but rather enriched by the new catholicity that emerges.

There is no doubt that Anglicanism currently stands at an important crossroads for its future identity. The *Windsor Report* is merely a signpost at this juncture (albeit an important one): it anticipates the process that is to come, but it cannot predict the outcomes. I agree with this assessment for the life of the Communion; it is too early to draw conclusions. However, we might say that the there are two very different versions of the Communion and its future that are beginning to emerge.

The first sees Anglicanism in concrete terms. The polity will be governed by law, and scripture will be its ultimate arbiter. Here, Anglicanism will become a tightly defined denomination in which intra-dependence is carefully policed. Diversity of belief, behaviour and practice will continue, but they will be subject to scrutiny and challenge.

The second sees Anglicanism as a more reflexive polity; one that has a shape, but is able to stretch and accommodate considerable diversity. Here the polity will be governed by grace, not law, and the Communion itself will continue to operate as both a sign and instrument of unity. Anglicanism will continue to be a defined form of ecclesial polity, but one that tolerates and respects the differences it finds within itself.

Personally, I pray and hope for option two. But I also pray that I will not be divided from my sisters and brothers who favour the first option. I pray that in the midst of our common and diverse struggles, we will discover ourselves afresh in the learning Church, within that community of peace we still know as the Anglican Communion. I believe that this may well stretch the Communion to its limits, and test its viability vigorously. But I believe the stretch will ultimately be worth it. For in reaching out just beyond ourselves, and moving outside our normal boundaries and comfort zones, God's own hand is already waiting to clasp our feeble groping.

8

The Grammar of Our Intercourse

DAVID STANCLIFFE

I

When the government in Great Britain were searching for a way in which to celebrate the second millennium and its achievements, they hit on the idea of a building a great dome in London to house the best of Britain. What was the iconic centrepiece to be? What they proposed was the source of those achievements – a working model of the human body with its bones, joints and organs. This proposal provoked me to do what I have rarely done: to write a letter to *The Times* to propose an alternative. Instead of seeking to answer the question 'How does the human body work?' I suggested that what was needed was something which asked that more important question: 'What is the human person for?' Contrasting the post-renaissance and Enlightenment obsession with the mechanics of how things work – the scientific and stereo-typically male question – with the important one of asking what human life is for, I proposed that they hang in the middle of the dome not some inflatable plastic doll, but an enormous crucifix.

The presumption of the modern, post-renaissance world is that the question most worth asking is how something works, whether it's the human body, a computer or your motor car, the Church of England or even the world itself. Armed with knowledge of how things work, we can conquer the world and answer every problem. But can we? The debates we have in public life over and over again show that we are moving inexorably into a position where a 'can' is assumed to imply a 'may', or perhaps even a 'should' if that will increase the sum of knowledge, or some other supposed good, like human longevity or increased wealth. If we can use our biological and scientific skills to alter the genetic make-up of the children of those who are carrying terrible diseases, of course we should, shouldn't we?

This might seem a debatable speculation, but I suspect that we unconsciously take for granted an engineering-style pattern of thinking where a 'can' assumes a 'may'. Patterns that derive from a precise, mechanistic language structure are ideal tools to use for examining how things – even the human body – work. But reflection on what things are for requires a more allusive, speculative mode, where contemplation and wonder may provide the key to unlock the mysteries, and where knowledge might give place to wisdom.

What follows has these questions in mind, and begins with some reflections on what the language we use does to our processes of experiencing, thinking and feeling.

II

I had an old-style classical education. Each week, as well as the books we were reading and the passages we had to translate from Latin and Greek unseen, we wrote versions in Latin and Greek prose and verse. We were set passages of English literature from widely different sources and had to turn them into something resembling the classical Latin of Cicero or Livy, or – if it were Greek – Demosthenes or Thucydides. For verse composition, Milton's *Paradise Lost* was a favourite for Latin hexameters, and I remember wrestling with turning some intractable Shelley into Greek iambics. Accuracy of the word for word kind of translation was scorned. Our efforts were judged mostly on the elegance of the syntax, how we had absorbed the idiom of the models or whether, in other words, we had got to the stage of actually thinking in the rhythms and prosody of the language we were imitating. Nor was it just in classical languages that these fiendish puzzles were set: I had a friend who in her finals was set a passage of P. G. Wodehouse to turn into – of all things – German prose.

The first task in turning a piece of English into Latin was to read it thoroughly, again and again. Most of the English passages we were set were the orotund prose of those writers who clearly liked the sound of their own voices, and you could imagine declaiming the passage like a latter-day Cicero. Turning Gibbon, Burke or Winston Churchill into Ciceronian Latin is not an impossible task. As you read a passage through, the task was to analyse it paragraph by paragraph to see if you could coax each paragraph into a single sentence. Classical Latin is constructed very tightly, and we were taught to analyse what was really going on: what was the central activity – the subject and the main verb – around which everything else could gather? Having established that, the task was to see where everything else fitted in. What was the temporal sequence of the events? Which sentences or phrases might become temporal antecedents, clauses that began with 'when'? or which were consequences, the 'so thats'? Could the relationship between one observation and the main sentence be expressed as a conditional clause, with an 'if', or even set negatively, 'in order that so-and-so should not happen ...' ? In the end, just such a complex web of aspirations, intentions and consequences – whether intended or not – was constructed, and the paragraph brought to a triumphant conclusion only by arriving at the last word – the main verb, which locked the preceding structure into place like the keystone of an arch.

I describe this in detail for those who have never had to do it to illustrate the quality of verbal engineering that is demanded. No matter how many sub-clauses and conditions, the whole thing has to hang together as a unified construction from which nothing can be lopped without losing the sense. Latin prose is the language in which Sir Humphrey speaks in *Yes, Minister*. When Jim Hacker tells Sir Humphrey, 'You are a moral vacuum', the latter offers a golden rule: 'Don't lift lids off cans of worms – everything is connected to everything else.'

Although the published speeches of Cicero – the Cataline Orations, for example – are clearly an edited and polished form of what was actually delivered, the basic rhetorical skill that was admired in classical Rome was the ability to hold in your mind whole arguments, and to marshal the facts to support them, in a logically ordered way that was not only plausible but unchallengeable. Winning an argument in the Roman Senate or in the Law Courts depended not only on possessing the facts and being able to marshal them in an order which was irrefutable but in having the forensic skills to anticipate your opponent's arguments and demolish them before he had a chance to use them.

At the heart of this process of tracking responsibility, apportioning blame and winning arguments – still the bed-rock of a lawyer's craft today – is the need to sort a cast-iron temporal sequence of events – of what happened first; of what was the cause or consequence of what; of what conditions are needed to be able to deduce with absolute certainty who was responsible for what. Again, the analogy is a mechanical one: imagine a complex machine, with pistons, cogwheels, rods and levers. Everything is connected to everything else, as Sir Humphrey said, and when you understand how each part of the process works, you can pull just one lever in the sure and certain knowledge that a can of ale or a secure conviction will be delivered at the other end.

And Latin is a marvellous language for doing this. The economy of the vocabulary, the precision of the constructions and above all the way in which the verbs are conjugated with a very precise sense of their temporality forges the chain of cause and effect into an indivisible whole.

But Greek 'is a foreign country; they do things differently there'.[1] Although the cultures share much, the languages differ in the way the verbs are conjugated and used. If Latin is the language of engineers and lawyers, Greek is the language of philosophers, of those who speculate and wonder. Of course there were great Greek lawyers like Demosthenes and Lysias; but the great Greek historian Thucydides offered a different take on the chain of cause and effect. Thucydides begins his great history of the Peleponesian War by laying out the presenting reasons why Athens went to war with Sparta. He promises to chronicle in detail the events that led to outbreak of hostilities, and later sets out the dispute between Corcyra and Corinth and all that followed from it. But at the outset[2] he declares that the real, the underlying reason that made war inevitable was that Sparta had become afraid of Athens' growing power. The answer he gives is not a mechanical or causal presenting one, but a psychological or analytical one, and it depends not on his precise analysis of the chain of cause and effect so much as on his overall judgement as to what is significant. There is a parallel here in the distinction between the different accounts of the creation in Genesis 1 – a Latin-style explanation of the chain of linear sequence – and that in Genesis 2 and 3, which offers a more Greek-style glimpse into why things are as they are, rather than a temporal account of how they came into being.

You do not have to read much Thucydides – or many Greek tragedies for that matter – to realize that the Greek language is less precise on temporal sequence and more suited to

---

1 L. P. Hartley: the famous opening sentence of his novel, *The Go-Between*.

2 Thucydides, *The Peleponesian War*, Book I, chapter 23.

describing the quality or style of the action. The way verbs conjugate may look as if there is as precise a boundary as there is in Latin between the past, the present and the future. But then you find that the present tense is used in a continuous historic sense; that the way you can talk about the past varies depending on the pastness of the past, the completion or not of that event, or whether the past is so vividly part of the present that the events of the past are best described as part of our experience now; that the degree of certainty that one can have about a possible future outcome can be expressed in a variety of moods: 'she might come' (in the subjunctive); 'I'd love her to come' (the optative); and – occasionally, and very vividly – 'she jolly well will come' (the future tense), let alone the shades between these, like 'she would have come', 'she might have come', 'I would have loved her to have come', or 'she may be coming' or even, right at the other end of the scale, 'she's about to come any moment'.

The moods as well as the tenses of classical Greek, provide a much more subtle way of describing the way objects, events and people react and inter-react. The subtlety of this verb system is developed still further in Russian, with its aspects – an almost built-in adverbial system; while in a different direction the substantial compound substantives of modern German serve to reify – to make one believe that a complex process has an actual existence independent of the interactions that are going on to develop the pattern of activity it describes in such compact shorthand – what in Russian or Greek would be a much more insubstantial and fluid process, using verbs rather than nouns to carry the sense of becoming.

Little wonder then that some languages are more useful for certain purposes and less useful for others. Perhaps more importantly, how far, I wonder, are we who are brought up to think in one language or language system – as we all are for our primary conceptual framework – aware of the limitations of our own first language system or of the differing possibilities for imaginative or conceptual thought in other languages we may come to learn?

III

Let me give an example of how these distinctions play out in the language of liturgy and the church buildings in which the liturgy is celebrated.[3]

In the West, the adoption of the basilical plan – of an essentially linear, aisled hall with a raised apse at the far end – has functional antecedents: this was the model of large public buildings available in the Roman empire, and the use of such buildings for the administration of justice made them both available and adaptable for use in public worship.

Unlike the house churches, which had little exterior sign that they were anything other than private houses, these buildings were essentially public, frequently with a colonnaded porch or entrance which proclaimed their accessibility. When used as law courts, the judge (acting in the Emperor's name) sat with his assessors on the bench that ran round the apse at one end of the building which was separated from the body of the hall by steps and a railing. Before them stood a table for the depositions and a bust of the Emperor with an incense burner on which a few grains were offered to show loyalty to the Emperor as the divine guarantor of justice, just as we swear to tell the truth on a copy of the Bible in a court of law today.

The Church adopted this basilical style for the majority of its religious buildings, preferring the basilica with a single apsidal end and the principal entrance on the short side opposite it to

---

3   For a fuller discussion of the different architectural settings of the liturgy in East and West, see David Stancliffe, *The Lion Companion to Church Architecture* (Oxford: Lion Hudson, 2008), esp., pp. 26–65.

the model of the pagan temple, which was largely a house for the image of the god. The liturgy soon adapted itself to these buildings, and in some ways there was an obvious continuity with the worship of the synagogue. A seat for the leader of the worship and an ambo – a raised platform with a desk to give audibility and visibility to the reader – were common to both. In other ways they were distinct. There was a *synthronon* or bench for the presbyters – the elders of the church – around the apse flanking the bishop's chair, sitting where the presiding judge and his assessors sat when a basilica was used as a court. At the head of the nave there came to be a railed area enclosed by low screens or *cancelli* (from which our word *chancel* ultimately derives) within which the various ministers of the liturgy, the deacons, readers and acolytes gathered. The *ambo*, sometimes an elaborate and lofty pulpit-like structure with a canopy and sometimes a raised platform with a reading desk, varied in position. In the Syrian church, it was usually a raised platform or *bema* in the middle of the nave where several ministers might gather to read the scriptures with people gathered round. In Justinian's great Hagia Sophia in Constantinople it formed a towering peninsular, jutting out into the central space and connected to the royal doors by an isthmus, a railed walkway or *solea*. Later in the West, the ambo was placed on one side or the other of the *cancelli*, or, as in the case of San Clemente in Rome, there was one on each side. From their place within the *cancelli*, the readers, cantor and deacon could have ready access to these places from which the scriptures could be easily heard. Most distinctive of all the interior features was the altar, and although there is some evidence to suggest that at first a wooden table was brought forward for the celebration of the sacrament only when it was needed, very soon a solid stone sarcophagus-like altar became the norm, frequently housed under a stone or wooden canopy or *ciborium*, in imitation of the canopies built over the shrine-tombs of the martyrs in the cemeteries.

Outside, there was frequently an *atrium* or forecourt with a fountain for a ritual washing which was sometimes linked with the baptistery. This baptistery was more than just a font: it continued to be a separate room for some centuries, as the majority of candidates for baptism were either adult, or adults with their households, and they went down into the waters of baptism naked, emerging to put on the white robe of their new life in Christ. The great processional Easter liturgy is easier to picture in the series of spaces around a basilica like that at Porec in Istria, or in San Clemente in Rome with its atrium than in the single church building we have become used to.

Behind this sense of processional movement up a longitudinally planned basilica lies a vision of our relationship to God which was to prove dominant in the West for some 800 years or more. This basilica functioned like a gigantic throne-room, with little to impede the progress of the worshipper towards the apsidal end. The worshipper is drawn into the procession – St Augustine called the whole of our eucharistic worship 'making the offering' – of the saints and martyrs of our faith. On the walls of the basilica of St Apollinare Nuovo in Ravenna (c. 490) the mosaic procession is led by the three magi in short tunics and close-fitting tights, dancing along on the tips of their toes as they make their way towards the throne at the apse, where God sits in majesty. If the vision is being summoned to attend the heavenly banquet, then the reality here and now is to join in the procession of those 'making the offering' and to take part in the foretaste of that banquet, the Holy Eucharist. Below the figure of Christ in the apse sits his earthly representative, the bishop, surrounded by his elders as Christ is surrounded by the apostles of the Church and the twenty-four elders of the Apocalypse. As the bishop moves from his throne in the apse to the altar, he is accompanied as

152

he takes the gifts by deacons, some bearing fans or *flabellae* – the Seraphim of Isaiah's vision. The liturgy is a linear succession of events, each stage unfolding from the last; and this is mirrored in a style of building which continued right through the great gothic churches with their series of spaces, one unfolding to the next as you move through the building from west to east, from darkness to light, from the sense of isolation and self-preoccupation to the foretaste of heaven itself.

By contrast, in Greek language and conceptual thought as well as in architecture, there is much less dependence on the linear, logical development of cause and effect, and much greater emphasis on the eternal present of the significant events of the past. The Orthodox liturgy is a making alive of that eternal action of God in Christ, so that the worshipper is drawn up into the ever-present continuity of the divine life, whereas in the West the sense of making the memorial, of the celebration of the Eucharist being a sequential series of recollections building towards a moment of revelation give a far more historicized and so linear sense. As the ways of thinking in the East and West couched in their different languages gradually diverged, so consequently did the styles of architectural expression. To simplify, Greek is the language of timeless, abstract reflection; Latin is the language of engineers and leverage; and both are exhibited in their respective buildings.

In the east, the essential building unit is a cube surmounted by a dome, expressing the welding of heaven to earth. To stand under the dome in an Eastern Church is to sense that you are in the place where heaven and earth are fused together, and this – emphasized by the lofty nature of Greek churches in relation to their length – gives a different dimension to the experience of worship. In a typical Greek church, the dome rises over a solid cross-shaped building, with a series of smaller domes over the apsidal ends of the aisles or the corners of the Greek cross plan. Although the eastern ends of the aisles may terminate with apses, the nave is hardly longer than the transepts or chancel, and is extended west by an arcaded narthex or porch. East of the central dome is the *templon,* the *cancelli* of Italian churches, the screens with a solid latticework base and pillars supporting a rail or beam such as can be seen in the Greek-inspired churches in the West like Grado or Torcello at the northern end of the Adriatic, to distinguish the presbytery. In time, this screen began to be hung with icons, and so developed into the solid structure with three doors that is familiar to us today in Orthodox churches as the *iconostasis.* In the transepts or wings of the central space are the lecterns for the cantors; at the head of the nave, among his people, is the bishop's throne, placed centrally in the Georgian tradition; and while the priest who celebrates the liturgy is often behind the iconostasis, only opening the royal doors to emerge and bless the congregation, the deacon is frequently among the people, not only for the proclamation of the gospel, but to offer their prayer in one of the many litanies that he sings.

IV

The distinction I am seeking to draw between these two models is primarily a difference in the processes of thinking – in the conceptual grammar – that different language makes possible rather than simply about our ability to translate accurately, which of course is a related, and more frequently rehearsed, topic.

Questions of translation do indeed raise interesting issues, as has recently come to the fore in the 2008 revision of the translation of the Roman Mass into English. The new translation of the Mass into English was commissioned in order to make it more faithful to the original Latin in which the Holy See published the Missa Normativa in 1967. The principle of dynamic equivalence, which requires a translator to know both the languages concerned and also to be able to use the prosody and idioms of the language into which the Latin is being translated, so that result actually sounds like English, might land up with an English translation that looks very different not only from a French translation but also from a translation into American.[4] This is deeply worrying to those who regard any signs of inculturation as disloyalty to the one, true expression of the rite in the Vatican's best Latin.

You touch on the same sensibilities in the Anglican tradition when someone alters the words of a well-known hymn. There are the – by now – well-accepted changes, like 'Hark! the herald angels sing' for 'Hark! how all the welkin rings', but a more striking example of a wilful alteration is in the third verse of Bishop Christopher Wordsworth's hymn *See the Conqueror mounts in triumph*:

> Thou hast raised our human nature
> > In the clouds to God's right hand;
> There we sit in heavenly places,
> > There with thee in glory stand;
> Jesus reigns, adored by angels;
> > Man with God is on the throne;
> Mighty Lord, in thine Ascension
> > We by faith behold our own.

This is clearly too strong meat for the editors of the modern *Hymns Old and New*,[5] who alter the sixth line to read: 'bears our

---

4   See for example Keith F. Pecklers SJ, *Dynamic Equivalence: The Living Language of Christian Worship* (Collegeville, IN: Liturgical Press, 2003).

5   *Hymns Old and New* is published by Kevin Mayhew, and is regularly updated. I may of course do the editors an injustice, attributing to them a westernizing theology which may be latent rather than

nature to the throne' and so offers an interesting example of the western, linear style of theology invading the bolder and more direct 'eastern' claim of Bishop Christopher Wordsworth's original.

The same sort of questions appear over different translations of the books of the Bible, where the boundary between translation and paraphrase opens huge questions about the translator's licence to interpret, let alone the rightness of importing twenty-first century phenomena like gender-consciousness into texts that stem from a very different era and culture. On the one hand you can argue that there can be no substitute for reading the texts in the language in which they were originally transmitted. The extreme of this thesis – revealing less than entirely pure motives – led to a remarkable peroration in a sermon one Christmas Day. An early nineteenth-century Dean of Christchurch, Thomas Gaisford, concluded his address to the townsfolk of Oxford with these words:

> Nor can I do better, in conclusion, than to urge upon you the study of the ancient tongues, which not only refines the intellect and elevates above the common herd but also leads not infrequently to positions of considerable emolument.[6]

On the other hand, the difficulty of accurate translation across both historical time-frames as well as cultural boundaries shows how advisable it is to have at least two versions before you, one more literal or conservative and one more free and

---

consciously in play. They may simply be trying to avoid the supposedly gender-specific 'man'.

6   Thomas Gaisford, 'Christmas sermon at Christ Church, Oxford', quoted by Hugh Lloyd-Jones in *Blood for the Ghosts* (Baltimore, MD: Johns Hopkins University Press, 1983), p. 82.

idiomatic, when the original language is inaccessible and you are trying to discover what the text might actually mean.

But what concerns me more than these much discussed examples centring round what constitutes translation are the unrecognised assumptions and misunderstandings that we make when we assume that languages operate in the same way, and that perfect translation will solve all our problems. This cannot be the case. There are some things that you simply cannot say – and therefore presumably even think – in certain languages: they just don't do it like that.

Let me give you a couple of examples: first, if you think in those German compound substantives, like *Vergang-enheitsbewältigung* – which we might roughly translate as 'coming to terms with the history of the past', a word used to describe how German people of our generation have had to deal with the consciousness that many of their immediate forebears did not foresee what the traumatic effects of collaboration or at least acquiescence with the Nazi regime have had – can you really get into George Herbert's poetry with its concrete imagery, its puns and nuanced verbs and its essentially understated, allusive way of making connections between visual, biblical and liturgical images? Or do you have to read him in English?

Second, there is British Sign Language, the sign language taught to and used by the profoundly deaf. When I was working with the Liturgical Commission, we had a visit from a group of the profoundly deaf and a number of chaplains who used BSL. They had asked to see us in order to impress on us the importance of crafting new liturgical texts that were as far as possible free from abstract terms and conceptual language; would we please write as far as possible in concrete terms and use vivid visual images.

As a worked example, we tried out on them some early drafts of Eucharistic Prayers that had been produced for use when children were present, of which we were rather proud, and received a kindly mark! Short sentences with a subject and a qualifying adjective, simple transitive verbs and an object were best; more than one adverb or adjective might muddy the water, and certainly no more than one link – a 'when' or an 'if', but not both – was as much syntax as would be comprehensible. Just imagine trying to turn St Paul's theology or the Athanasian Creed into BSL!

V

Historically, it was Latin, with its terse economy, its comparatively small vocabulary and its very highly developed sense of linear temporal sequence, that in the medieval period became the European language in which the law was practised and in which Thomist theology was developed. Our present legal system, in which facts are adduced, chronology determined and the chains of cause and effect established, owes much to the logic of classical Latin prose and the type of thinking that it allows – or even encourages. Within the webs of action and interaction, chronologies can be established, responsibilities can be allocated and the coherence of emerging patterns tested against case law – as the accumulated corpus of precedent is called – and so the outcome of the case can be predicted. Judgements quote precedent extensively, and the tight logic of the way in which the case is built up gives the barrister a fair idea as to whether he will win his case or not.

The same essentially linear processes have come to be the way in which the Roman Catholic Church has done its theology. The process is highly deductive, and the arguments have a linear quality, which leads – even today – to a particular style of reasoning. I illustrate my reservation with this mental furniture as the only or dominant model within which to think theologically by reference to comments on the Papal Encyclical *Ut unum sint* – That they May Be One.[7]

Ut unum sint was a renewed plea for Christian unity, particularly directed towards the Orthodox churches. The encyclical acknowledges that in baptism Christians become members of the Body of Christ, and that many churches have some (or most) of the elements of truth which, however, the encyclical claims exists in its fullness only in the Roman Catholic Church. The encyclical's positive and forward-looking tone is encouraging, but the model for unity remains essentially structural, rather than anthropological. There is a logical, linear sequence of mechanical links, each dependant on the previous one till they are validly rooted in Christ. After quoting the document *Unitatis Redintegratio* from the Second Vatican Council which speaks of the Roman See acting as 'a moderator', and recognizing that the ministry of unity which is historically a particular responsibility of the Bishop of Rome is to be at the service of the Church (§95), Pope John Paul stated that 'the communion of the particular churches with the Church of Rome, and of their Bishops with the Bishop of Rome, is – in God's plan – an essential requisite of full and visible communion' (§96). And here this great and unbreakable chain becomes to outsiders apparently circular. For unity there must be communion, for communion there must be unity of ministry, since sharing in communion is the sign of being in communion, not a means to achieve it: 'it is not a substitute for unity, but the fruit of unity.' For those outside the Roman Catholic Church it seems extremely difficult to break into this charmed circle. In relationships with other churches, especially the Scandinavian Lutheran Churches, the practice of intercommunion has played a considerable part in bringing the

---

7   *Ut unum sint* (That They May Be One). Papal Encyclical by Pope John Paul II published in June 1995.

churches together. But the difficulty lies in the fact that acceptance of one another's sacraments implies acceptance of one another's orders as a logically prior link in the chain of authenticity, of expressing the mind of Christ.

One way forward might be to press the claims of a model of authenticity – of a truly apostolic ministry – which was less linear; not so much of a mechanical linkage to guarantee the uninterrupted transmission of *potestas*, of priestly power to consecrate, as a raft or web. I think of it like this: we have a hammock which seems able to bear the weight of our heaviest friends, yet is made entirely of wool. Its secret lies in the fact that it has an enormous number of strands, not one of which is bearing more than a fraction of the weight, and strand is woven to strand laterally as well as lengthwise; it has – if I recall the terms correctly – both warp and weft.

Such a web-like model of apostolic ministry might look more like this:

> Apostolicity belongs to the whole church living in continuity with the faith and mission of the Apostles. Succession in the episcopal ministry is a visible and personal way of focussing and of signifying the apostolicity of the whole church. The apostolicity and continuity of the whole church is inextricably bound up with the apostolicity and continuity of its ordained ministry, focussed in episcopal ministry. Continuity in the episcopate signifies God's promise to be faithful to his church. At the same time, it signifies the Church's intention to be faithful to its apostolic calling. It gives assurance to the faithful that the Church today intends to do and to be what it has always intended to do and to be. The laying on of hands by bishops in succession is a sign – an effective sign – of that intention, but continuity is also manifested in ordered succession in the historic episcopal sees of the catholic church.

> Apostolic succession in the Church should therefore be seen as
> a rope of several strands.[8]

That certainly is how the Porvoo Declaration – a statement of common understanding which lays a path open for the interchange of ministries between the Churches of the Anglican Communion in Europe and the Lutheran Churches of the Baltic and Scandinavia – understands the historical episcopal succession.

But in the thinking of Pope John Paul II, it is the communion of the bishops of other churches with the Bishop of Rome that is an essential requisite of full and visible communion; and that communion of bishops implies both a recognition of authenticity and an acceptance of authority. Over the centuries, the unity and authenticity of the Church has come to centre more on the guarantee of apostolic origin than on the presence of apostolic life. But the apostolic note remains crucial. The unity of the church is a particular concern for the bishop just because the tradition focuses the responsibility for handing on the faith together with keeping the Church together in him: the unity of the Church is sustained by a community of faith which stretches over the ages. This is made clear at an ordination, where the bishop does not act alone: his presbyters must be with him and the Eucharist celebrated. In the *Apostolic Tradition*[9] the bishop is simultaneously the *alter Christus* and the *alter apostolus*. While the bishop alone can, like Christ, 'give' the ministry, the presbyters accompany him in this giving as a visible sign of the new community, where past, present and future are imaged in the eucharistic foretaste of the Kingdom. The implication is

---

8   *The Porvoo Common Statement* (London: Council for Christian Unity of the General Synod of the Church of England, 1993).

9   *The Apostolic Tradition*, formerly ascribed to Hippolytus, §3.

161

that apostolic continuity is realized through the bishop, not as an individual but as the focus of a continuing community of faith. Apostolic succession through episcopacy is essentially a succession of Church structure. How else after all can the ordained ministry receive Christ's authority if not through the Church? Any 'apostolic succession' which by-passes communion, the essential corporate-making ingredient in building the Church as a body which is continuous in space and time, is vulnerable. It is rooted only in the single link of a massive chain which binds it clearly, but potentially disastrously – if one link snaps, the whole chain breaks – to its origin in the past. Communion, of which the Eucharist is the type and origin, is more like a web, a net, a hammock. In the Eucharist past and future, heaven and earth, God and humanity are bound together in Christ, the unique source of the Church's ministry.

> [Christ] is before all things, and in him all things hold together. He is the head of the body, the church; he is the beginning, the first-born from the dead, that in everything he might be pre-eminent. For in him all the fullness of God was pleased to dwell, and through him to reconcile to himself all things (Colossians 1.17-19).

This unity is the essence of God's nature, and whether we think of Christ as the one who reconciles us to God, or the one who inaugurates the new creation, or embodies the Kingdom, the implication is clear in the high-priestly prayer in John's Gospel:

> I do not pray for these only, but also for those who believe in me through their word, that they may all be one; even as thou, Father, art in me, and I in thee, that they also may be in us, so that the world may believe that thou hast sent me. The glory which thou hast given me I have given to them, that they may be one even as we are one, I in them and thou in me, that they

may be perfectly one, so that the world may know that thou
hast sent me and hast loved them even as thou hast loved me
(John 17.20-23).

At the heart of this model of unity is a repetitive, circular
model of mutual indwelling, a pattern of communion. Our
participation in the divine life, our communion with God, is by
incorporation into Christ's one, perfect self-offering to the
Father; and what exhibits, what reveals, the divine glory is this
perfect union – with God, with one another, and – we might
add in a post-Freudian age – with ourselves and the natural
order, (though the latter might be foreign to St John). It is this
two-way relationship between Christ and the Father which we
enter when we are baptized and which is at the heart of priestly
ministry. Christ reveals the Father to us, and offers our
worship to the Father. 'In the Eucharist', declares the Moscow
Statement,[10] 'the eternal priesthood of Christ is constantly
manifested in time. The presiding celebrant in the liturgical
action has a twofold ministry: as an icon of Christ, acting in
the name of Christ, towards the community and also as a
representative of the community expressing the priesthood of
the faithful.'

This may seem an over-heavy sledge-hammer with which to
crack a nut, but this reflection on the contrast between the
logical, linear, Latin-style chain of thinking in the Roman
Church and the more circular, relational, web-like pattern of
reflection that the Anglican (and indeed Orthodox) tradition
espouses, illustrates well the conceptual differences which
often make it difficult for the partners in a conversation to hear
one another.

If the argument over the nature of the unity of the Church
can only be conceived in linear terms, then of course a

---

10   The Moscow agreed statement of the Anglican–Orthodox dialogue
     (1976).

mechanical connection to the see of Rome that guarantees uniformity of belief and practice and a crystal-clear line of authority will be the only solution that gives a watertight guarantee.

But are different models that derive from other linguistic thought patterns possible? Would it be possible to think that unity – like that experienced by the infant Church on the day of Pentecost – might have more to do with the complementarity of different languages, patterns of expression and thought-forms rather than in a historical or imposed uniformity? The phenomenon of different languages was certainly understood in the Hebrew Testament (Genesis 11.1-9) as a sign of disunity, leading to chaos. But it is exactly this same phenomenon that is discovered to be a sign of the unity of the Church in mission in Acts 2.1-13. True, neither the day of Pentecost nor the common life of the Christians of Corinth sound like tidy expressions of the apostolic Church, but they – like the organic models of the Church which figure in the earlier writings of the New Testament – are a good deal more vivacious than the later and more structural expressions of he life of the Church in writings like the Letter to the Ephesians (2.19-22).

On a different level, the Anglican Communion – hitherto the great ecclesial gift to the divided churches as an exemplar of how to manage unity in and through diversity – is currently engaged in a not dissimilar exercise in unity to which the assumed solution is to provide a Covenant into which different Provinces can enter. This 'Covenant', couched in a long document setting out expected loyalties and ways of behaving, looks suspiciously like a contract, not a covenant, and is clearly designed to set down in juridical terms limits to the boundaries of what is acceptable behaviour. Hitherto, the Communion has been defined in relational terms: relation to the office of the Archbishop of Canterbury, and his invitation to participate in a conference every decade; relation to a style of worship; a way of relating to the biblical documents, the historic Creeds and the ordered life as expressed in the historic, threefold ministry. It is about what we have done together and the way in which we have done it, especially in church. In short, the adverbs of our common life are being replaced by substantives. If, in a married relationship, the ways of kindliness and graciousness, of affection and trust, have become so eroded that lists of duties and agreed standards of behaviour had to be substituted for attentive and loving response, then we wonder if the marriage still exists except on paper.

What concerns me is that differences in understanding may come to be based less on our attempts to enter into the mind of Christ – indeed, when people from different traditions gather, study, pray and eat together remarkable things can happen – and more upon the ways of thinking that the use of one particular language structure encourages. Intellectually, we know that this is an area worthy of exploration; practically and emotionally we find it hard to do, which is why that part of the bishop's ministry which is about engaging with the leaders and thinkers in other intellectual traditions and with Christians who do their theology in other languages is so vital for the Church's pursuit of the truth, as well as of the unity of the local church with the Church universal.

VI

What does this analysis lead us to believe we can trust in the difficult but vital process of sharing our thoughts, or even of sensing another's feelings? Of course we must attend to the skills and processes of those who labour to make translations, and be aware of the philological, philosophical and hermeneutic questions raised by the processes of translating that are explored by such radically different thinkers as George

Steiner[11] and Paul Ricoeur[12]. But in the end, however sophisticated the processes of translation, there remains a basic question about communication between two persons: even if we go to the same Verdi opera together, eat the same meal afterwards and then look at the same night sky, how can we know – whatever language we use – that we are sharing the same thoughts or experience? When we embark on the all-important processes of knowing and being known which form the basis of our mutual relationships, what can we trust? How can we relate these considerations of how the grammar of our intercourse is formed to the exploration of the formation and development of the imagination? What creates and stretches the hinterland of our minds? What part, for example, is played by communication systems other than the verbal? What do we owe to the imaginative longings, to the optative mood, as it would be known in Greek? Does my desire to be understood, or for illumination, or for the healing of a relationship or for a person actually alter who I am becoming or jump over the physical void to another person, like a spark in a plug?

While it is not possible to make an exhaustive exploration of this vast subject, non-verbal communication certainly deserves to be recognized. This is not the place for a long excursus on the origins of art, but it is worth noting an important recent study by David Lewis-Williams[13] of the emergence in the late Ice Age of the animal art in the limestone caves of France. He links neurological insights with anthropological research to provide a joined-up explanation how becoming what the

---

11 George Steiner, *After Babel: Aspects of Language and Translation* (Oxford and New York: Oxford University Press, 1975).

12 Paul Ricoeur, *On Translation*, translated by Eileen Brennan, with an Introduction by Richard Kearney (London and New York: Routledge, 2006).

13 David Lewis-Williams, *The Mind in the Cave* (London: Thames and Hudson, 2002).

Welsh poet David Jones called 'the maker of signs'[14] was a key moment in becoming human.

Interesting work is being done by scientists like Susan Greenfield[15] in a number of interrelated disciplines on what is happening to human imagination in a world where most of those now growing up in the western world have such an exposure to rapidly changing visual stimuli on Internet, television, film and video game that some of the pathways which have 'joined up the dots' in the brain laterally – to use a layman's language – seem to be in danger of withering. Are children's brains actually being altered by the Internet and television? Think of what happens when you make a television production of a classic English novel by Hardy or Trollope. What may occupy three or four pages in the novel, describing the long walk home through the slow dusk after a heavy day's work, is reduced to a four-second pan. Nothing of the slowly fading light, the footsteps more leaden with each passing minute, the aching shoulders and the anticipation of a welcoming fire: just a mood flash before the next action.[16] And how do you convey, simply in visual terms, the evocative smell of wet earth after a shower of rain? Or the feel of a violin bow on a gut string? Do today's children notice birdsong as they go jogging with their ipods? How do they register the smell of

---

14 In David Jones *Epoch and Artist* (London, Faber & Faber, 1959).

15 See Susan Greenfield, *Tomorrow's People: How 21st-century Technology is Changing the Way we Think and Feel* (London: Allen Lane 2003).

16 There is much to be learnt from the processes of turning a novel into a film script. See the interesting discussion in the Foreword, Preface and Introduction to Anthony Minghella's film script of Michael Ondaatje's novel: *The English Patient* (London: Methuen Drama, 1997) where the film, which I saw first, is stunning visually, dramatically and evocatively, but where whole swathes of the marvellous novel are entirely absent. What parts of our imagination are stretched by each creation?

fresh milk or a peat fire? Do they still make imaginary pictures in their heads from the books they have read? What about the senses of touch and sensitivity to texture? In particular, what about the seeing that comes from looking at the same landscape or altarpiece day after day in all seasons and lights – that slow imprint of a sense of place that builds up a feeling of being at home? There is seeing – as in the daily encounter with the ikon before which you say your prayers but which you never really look at, certainly not as a work of art, and seeing – as in the cursory glance at an Italian *trecento* panel that you have paid to walk past on the walls of the Uffizi in Florence. In the former, there is a slow build-up of impressions that relate to the moods of your emotional experience and the deepening quality of your spiritual life, in the latter, there is a conscious desire to get something out of the momentary encounter – after all, you have come a long way and paid to see it so need to feel that the time and expense have been (note the past tense) worth it. Is this where the gospel warning 'that they may indeed look, but not perceive, and may indeed listen, but not understand' (Mark 4.12) comes into its own?

Are there parallels here with the necessary limitations imposed by the binary, on/off, yes/no system that is the basis of all computer technology? When you blow up an image taken by a digital camera, however sophisticated, the pixels come out with straight edges: how does what we know about the importance of curves in giving life even to apparently straight line fit with this? There is not one straight line in that masterpiece of classical architecture, the Parthenon on the Acropolis in Athens. Nor is there one in Lutyens's Cenotaph in Whitehall. Similarly, singing to the accompaniment of an electronic organ is always a battle. This is because their sound is produced in perfect, solid chunks. The notes do not have – as the notes produced by the human voice, or an oboe or a pipe organ do – a plosive beginning, a blossoming growth and a tailed-off end, which gives each note its own, individual life. Can the mechanical means, by which so much of our experience is replicated and shared, ever give us the real thing? And can this virtual reality, so immediately accessible, replace the formation and cultivation of our own imagination? And if it can, do we want it to?

To take a particular case, what is the present-day equivalent of the processes behind the monastic formation practised between the fifth and twelfth centuries? I had always been puzzled as to how Bernard of Clairvaux, the instigator of the Cluniac reforms, could have preached such exotic sermons on the Song of Songs with their rich and imaginative imagery at the same time as he was making the interiors of his great Abbey Churches like Fontenay and Pontigny so austere architecturally and so plain decoratively, forbidding all stained glass, figurative carving and painting, until I learnt[17] that he wanted his monks to make their own imaginative hinterland by using the techniques of classical rhetoric – filing away associations and images that illuminated the scripture-based patterns of association and typology – for themselves, making their own 'files' as we would call them, and indexing them in a mental pigeon-hole system in the same way as a jurist in preparing a case to argue before the courts in classical times would have memorized the arguments to be used to counter his opponent's points, whenever produced. Is something like this what our computers do for our thinking as well as for disciplining our thought-processes today?

---

17 See Mary Carruthers, *The Craft of Thought: Meditation, Rhetoric, and the Making of Images, 400-1200* (Cambridge: Cambridge University Press, 1998).

VII

The interim conclusions I draw from these reflections are as follows. First, there is much more work to be done on how different people think, dream and imagine when they become conscious of their basic imaginative equipment. Do those languages which are written in pictograms, for example, enable a richer and more visual imaginative hinterland?

Second, we need to know more about what enables emotional, and not just conceptual, intelligence. At what point, and by what mechanisms do feelings and longings actually alter how we do our thinking? What place does empathy play? Do identical twins, who so often seem to intuit what each other is thinking, have some 'wiring' which enables thought processes to be mirrored in their brains?

Further reflection on the language of music, for example, and the language of love might reveal not verbal languages which none the less convey sophisticated messages – even to those whose technical knowledge of music – say – is pretty limited.

The language of art and music, the language of spatial relationship and silence, the half-stated language of poetry, suggestion and allusion, as well as the language of the seriously disturbed and mentally ill all seem to point to a series of layers of meaning, which range from the 'plain meaning', a literal reading of the text, to a highly complex and sophisticated hermeneutic of interpretation, ranging from Patristc typology to the word triggering described by Murray Cox and Alice Thielgaard[18] in their work with the patients at Broadmore.

I am interested in how there reflections help us to understand each other better, when conversations take place

---

18 Murray Cox and Alice Thielgaard, *Mutative Metaphors in Psychotherapy: The Aeolian Mode* (London: Jessica Kingsley, 1997).

between those of apparently differing religious convictions, and in particular in how we learn to listen more attentively and less judgementally.

Index